# COUNTRIES OF THE WORLD

# Indonesia

Gareth Stevens Publishing
**MILWAUKEE**

**About the Author:** Frederick Fisher is a travel writer and novelist living in the United States. He and his wife have adventured extensively in Southeast Asia, and they spend six months on the Pacific Rim each year.

Written by
**FREDERICK FISHER**

Edited by
**GERALDINE MESENAS**

Designed by
**HASNAH MOHD ESA**

Picture research by
**SUSAN JANE MANUEL**

First published in North America in 2000 by
**Gareth Stevens Publishing**
1555 North RiverCenter Drive, Suite 201
Milwaukee, Wisconsin 53212 USA

For a free color catalog describing
Gareth Stevens' list of high-quality books
and multimedia programs, call
1-800-542-2595 (USA) or
1-800-461-9120 (CANADA).
Gareth Stevens Publishing's
Fax: (414) 225-0377.

© **TIMES EDITIONS PTE LTD 2000**
Originated and designed by
Times Editions Pte Ltd
Times Centre, 1 New Industrial Road
Singapore 536196
http://www.timesone.com.sg/te

**Library of Congress Cataloging-in-Publication Data**
Fisher, Frederick.
Indonesia / by Frederick Fisher.
p. cm. — (Countries of the world)
Includes bibliographical references and index.
Summary: Introduces the geography, history, government, commerce, people, and culture of the Republic of Indonesia, an archipelago made up of thousands of islands.
ISBN 0-8368-2317-6 (lib. bdg.)
1. Indonesia — Juvenile literature. [1. Indonesia] I. Title. II. Series: Countries of the world (Milwaukee, Wis.)
DS615.F54    2000
959.8—dc21            99-34978

Printed in Malaysia

1 2 3 4 5 6 7 8 9 04 03 02 01 00

# Contents

**5 AN OVERVIEW OF INDONESIA**

6 Geography
10 History
16 Government and the Economy
20 People and Lifestyle
28 Language and Literature
30 Arts
34 Leisure and Festivals
40 Food

**43 A CLOSER LOOK AT INDONESIA**

44 Borobudur
46 The Chinese-Indonesians
48 Cockfights and Bullfights
50 East Timor
52 Ecology and the Burning Forest
54 Gamelan Music
56 Java Man
58 Orangutans
60 *Ramayana* and *Mahabharata*
62 The Rise and Fall of Suharto
64 The Spice Islands
66 The Toradja
68 Traditional Dress
70 Wayang Kulit
72 Wedding Traditions

**75 RELATIONS WITH NORTH AMERICA**

*For More Information ...*
86 Full-color map
88 Black-and-white reproducible map
90 Indonesia at a Glance
92 Glossary
94 Books, Videos, Web Sites
95 Index

# AN OVERVIEW OF INDONESIA

The Republic of Indonesia is the largest country in Southeast Asia. It is an archipelago made up of thousands of islands scattered at the junction of four major bodies of water — the Pacific Ocean, the Indian Ocean, the Celebes Sea, and the South China Sea. Indonesia is a natural paradise of lush rain forests, soaring volcanic peaks, and sandy sea coasts, as well as an urban landscape of skyscrapers, ghettos, and ongoing construction.

Throughout its history, Indonesia has endured imperialism, revolutions, military brutality, natural disasters, and civil wars. Today, Indonesians face tough economic times, intense political struggles, and waves of invading tourists.

*Opposite:* **Balinese traditional dances feature elaborate costumes and controlled movements.**

*Below:* **The** *bajaj* **(BAH-jaj) is a common form of public transportation in Jakarta.**

## THE FLAG OF INDONESIA

The Indonesian national flag is called Sang Dwiwarna (sahng dwee-WAHR-nah), or the Bicolor. It is made up of two bands — white and red. The white band symbolizes justice and purity, and the red band symbolizes gallantry and freedom. The flag is hoisted in front of the presidential palace, government buildings, and Indonesian missions abroad. In 1945, after World War II, Indonesia declared its independence, and the Bicolor was first flown amidst Japanese forces. Indonesian independence, however, was confirmed four years later in 1949, when the Bicolor was officially declared the national flag of the new republic.

# Geography

## The Land

Indonesia is made up of 13,670 islands, only half of which are inhabited. The country shares the large island of Borneo with the two Malaysian states of Sabah and Sarawak and the Kingdom of Brunei. The island of New Guinea is split between the Indonesian province of Irian Jaya and the island country of Papua New Guinea. Jakarta, situated on the island of Java, is Indonesia's capital and largest city. Indonesia consists of twenty-seven provinces. It is the fourth most populous country in the world, after China, India, and Russia.

*Below:* **Many mountains in Indonesia are active volcanoes. One is Mount Sinabung in Sumatra, which spews smoke and ash from time to time.**

The map of Indonesia (see pages 86–87) resembles the scattered pieces of a jigsaw puzzle. The islands of Sumatra, Java, Timor, and other southern islands curve around Kalimantan and Celebes like a quarter moon. The Moluccas Islands are dispersed throughout central Indonesia, while Irian Jaya is anchored on the eastern end of the Indonesian archipelago. Peninsular Malaysia lies east of Sumatra, across the Strait of Malacca, with Singapore at its southern tip; the Philippines lies just north of the Moluccas. Australia is directly south of the Indonesian archipelago.

# Mother Nature's Blessing and Curse

Indonesia is a land of natural beauty. The country has more beaches than any other country in the world. Bali, with its famous beaches of either black or white sand, has long been a popular tourist destination. Coral formations support biodiverse undersea gardens that attract divers and snorkelers to the archipelago.

The fertile plains of Sumatra, Java, Borneo, and Irian Jaya are the backbone of Indonesian agriculture, its most important economic sector. The main crop is rice, the staple food of Indonesians and many other Asian peoples.

Natural disasters plague the country. The islands of Indonesia are lined with beautiful mountains, many of which are active volcanoes. Indonesia is also prone to earthquakes. In 1992, a massive earthquake struck the island of Flores, destroying villages and killing over two thousand people. In February 1994, a severe earthquake occurred in Sumatra, killing 180 people.

*Left:* **Rural life on Bali presents an idyllic picture — a land of forests, rice fields, soaring volcanic peaks, and sandy sea coasts. Indian leader Mahatma Gandhi of India once described Bali as "the morning of the world."**

## Seasons

Located close to the Equator, Indonesia has a tropical climate, with monsoon seasons. The wet season lasts from November to March, and the dry season lasts from June to October. Between the monsoon seasons, temperatures range from 74° to 88° Fahrenheit (23° to 31° Celsius).

Rainfall is extremely heavy. Some mountainous regions may have up to 240 inches (610 centimeters) of rain each year. The lowlands average 70 to 125 inches (178 to 318 cm) of rain. Hardly any rain falls from June to October, and Indonesia's rain forests become dry and prone to fires. When the summer monsoon rains finally arrive in November, the forests rapidly become lush and green again. During this period of heavy rains, large areas of eastern Sumatra, southern Borneo, and Java are inundated. Mangrove swamps and marshy forests steam up because of the heat and poor drainage. Swamp vegetation survives by balancing on long stilt roots.

Temperatures are lower in mountainous regions. Puncak Jaya in Irian Jaya remains snowcapped throughout the year.

*Above:* **Braving the heavy rains, a resourceful Indonesian girl uses a banana leaf as a makeshift umbrella.**

### ECOLOGY AND THE BURNING FOREST

In recent years, the effects of El Niño — an abnormal weather condition that causes extremes in world climates — and the slash-and-burn methods of Indonesian farmers in Kalimantan and other parts of Indonesia have created huge clouds of smothering smog. The haze floats as far as Malaysia and Singapore.

(*A Closer Look, page 52*)

# Plants and Animals

Indonesia is home to a huge variety of plants. Giant trees, ferns, mosses, lichens, palms, bamboo, vines, and creepers fill the forests. Carnivorous pitcher plants are large enough to trap and "eat" small animals. Some trees, such as the ketapang, reach heights of over 200 feet (61 meters). From the branches of tall trees, the seeds of strangler figs send long tendril roots to the ground. As the fig grows, it gradually strangles its host tree — hence the name. Vines aptly named *wait-a-while* or *wait-a-bit* are tipped with spines that catch at people hiking the jungle trails. Native flower species include dozens of varieties of orchids.

Many species of mammals, reptiles, and birds live in the Indonesian rain forest. Primates are found on many of the islands. Small, saucer-eyed tarsiers are found on the Sulawesi and Sunda islands, while langurs and proboscis monkeys live on Borneo. Gibbons and orangutans can also be found in the jungles of Borneo and Sumatra. Tigers, leopards, panthers, and smaller jungle cats roam the larger islands. Reptiles are plentiful in the forests and swamps. Birdwatchers have an exhausting list of rare and almost extinct species to observe. Swarms of butterflies and moths flash in the depths of the forests like flowers and jewels.

*Above:* **The world's largest flower is the *Rafflesia arnoldii*, which is found in the jungles of Sumatra and Borneo. It blooms only for a few days and is also called the stinking corpse lily because it attracts insects with an odor similar to that of rotting flesh.**

*Left:* **The Komodo dragon is found on the island of Komodo. It can grow up to 10 feet (3 m) long and weigh up to 176 pounds (80 kilograms).**

## ORANGUTANS

**The endangered orangutan is found in Borneo and Sumatra. Many conservation programs have been established in Indonesia to ensure the survival of these wonderful, intelligent animals.**

(*A Closer Look*, page 58)

# History

During the neolithic period, groups of people from Asia, called the Proto-Malays, settled on the Indonesian islands. Chinese and Indian traders came to Indonesia in the fifth century A.D. In the ninth century, two great kingdoms ruled Central Java — the Sailendra dynasty and the Mataram dynasty. In 1294, the Majapahit kingdom grew to prominence and claimed sovereignty over much of what is now Indonesia and Malaysia.

## The Rise of Islam and the Spice Trade

Arab traders brought Islam to Indonesia in the seventh century. By the sixteenth century, many Indonesian states had adopted Islam. The spread of Islam was mainly due to the rise in the China-India spice trade, which attracted Muslim traders from the Middle East and Malacca, a port in the Malay Peninsula. In 1511, the Portuguese captured the major trading center of Malacca, from which they sought to control the spice trade. The British and Dutch were not far behind, hoping to gain a foothold in the profitable spice trade. Their arrival in Southeast Asia signaled a turning point in Indonesian history.

**JAVA MAN**

Humans may have originated in Indonesia. Java Man was found in the river valleys of central Java. Other traces of early humans have also been found in the Indonesian archipelago. Crude stone implements and ancient cave paintings proved that a rudimentary civilization once existed in Indonesia.
*(A Closer Look, page 56)*

*Below:* **The Prambanan temple complex, constructed by the Mataram dynasty, forms the largest group of Hindu temples in Indonesia.**

## The Dutch and the Ethical Policy

In 1602, the Dutch East India Company arrived in Indonesia. By 1619, Jan Pieterszoon Coen, governor-general of the Dutch East Indies, had established the capital in Jakarta and renamed it *Batavia*. The Dutch rapidly emerged as a major player in the spice trade to Europe.

In 1800, the Dutch East India Company went bankrupt, and the Dutch government took control of its territories in Indonesia. The Dutch introduced coffee and other crops to Indonesia and made it compulsory for one-fifth of all cultivable land to be used for export crops. By the end of the nineteenth century, the remaining islands of the archipelago were brought under Dutch control, and all of Indonesia became a Dutch colony.

In the early 1900s, the Dutch government introduced the Ethical Policy, which provided funds to establish agriculture, health, and education systems in the archipelago. Although not all the goals of the Ethical Policy were met, it helped improve roads, railroads, and shipping. More importantly, however, it led to the development of a small group of Western-educated native Indonesians, who brought their nationalistic ideals home and agitated the native Indonesian masses to revolt.

*Above:* **The Dutch lived lavishly in large households with many Indonesian servants.**

**THE SPICE ISLANDS**

The Maluku, or Moluccas, an age-old source of cloves, nutmeg, and other spices, attracted traders from the Middle East, China, India, and Europe as early as 300 B.C. Today, the islands attract tourists to their tropical rain forests and incredible beaches and reefs.

*(A Closer Look, page 64)*

# Nationalism and World War II

In 1927, the Indonesian Nationalist Party (PNI) was established under the leadership of native Indonesian Sukarno, a charismatic, Western-educated engineer. In 1929, he was arrested by the Dutch for his political activities. Released two years later, he began expounding his theories of independence for Indonesia. In 1933, the Dutch arrested him again and exiled him to Bengkulu on Sumatra.

The Japanese invaded Indonesia in 1942, driving out the Dutch. Sukarno struck a deal with the Japanese — he would help them in the war against the Allies, and, in return, they would allow him to promote nationalism. Sukarno declared Indonesia's independence as soon as the Japanese surrendered on August 17, 1945, and proclaimed himself president. It took four more years of struggle with the returning Dutch before they relinquished sovereignty in 1949. Sukarno's dreams of an independent Indonesia were realized.

*Left:* **On December 27, 1949, Queen Juliana of the Netherlands signed the act transferring sovereignty of the colony to the Independent Republic of the United States of Indonesia. Former Indonesian prime minister Mohammad Hatta is seated to the right of Queen Juliana.**

## Sukarno's Guided Democracy

As head of state, Sukarno strengthened his position by dissolving all political parties. In 1957, he instituted his so-called "Guided Democracy" and soon dissolved the elected parliament. His power relied on his alliance with the military. Sukarno did not get along well with the United States and other Western powers. Yet his dictatorial reign continued. He finally compelled the Dutch to cede West Irian (Irian Jaya) in 1963. Two years later, Sukarno took Indonesia out of the United Nations.

## General Suharto

A general by the name of Suharto led the army's strategic command during this period. He brutally suppressed a revolt in March, 1966. He also persuaded Sukarno to retire and took over the leadership of the country. The new order, with Suharto in charge, ruled from 1966 to May, 1998. He took a pro-Western stance and settled long-standing conflicts with Malaysia. Suharto was a key figure in the formation of the Association of Southeast Asian States (ASEAN), which promotes cooperation and trade relations with the West. Indonesia was resurfacing as an international power.

*Above:* **ASEAN leaders meet annually to work toward the association's objectives to stimulate economic growth, cultural development, and social progress. The picture above shows Suharto (*second from left*) with the leaders of Brunei, Malaysia, the Philippines, Singapore, and Thailand in 1992.**

**THE RISE AND FALL OF SUHARTO**

**Born near Yogyakarta, Suharto became Indonesia's second president in 1968. In May 1998, he resigned amidst the bloody riots that arose as a result of the 1997 economic crisis.**

(A Closer Look, page 62)

# The Economic Crisis of 1997

In 1997, a major economic recession hit Southeast Asia, and the rupiah, Indonesia's currency, collapsed. The International Monetary Fund (IMF), an agency of the United Nations, pledged to assist Indonesia in its time of need. In return, the Indonesian government was required to implement certain humanitarian and economic programs.

Meanwhile, President Suharto, his family, and his close friends were accused of corruption. During Suharto's presidency, increasing unemployment and poverty caused great unrest among the Indonesian people. In May 1998, riots, ethnic violence, and other atrocities occurred in Jakarta and Medan, and hundreds of people were killed. Foreign investors fled the country, as did the ethnic Chinese, who controlled a large proportion of the Indonesian economy and were targets of racial attacks. On May 21, 1998, amidst the riots, Suharto resigned in favor of Bacharuddin Jusuf Habibie, his vice-president.

**EAST TIMOR**

**East Timor remained a Portuguese colony until 1975, when the Indonesian government forcefully annexed it to the republic. Since then, thousands of Timorese have died in clashes with the Indonesian army.**
(*A Closer Look, page 50*)

*Below:* **Student demonstrations were a common sight during the chaos of May 1998.**

## Sukarno (1901–1970)

The paramount leader of Indonesia's nationalist movement and the country's first president (from 1945 to 1968), Sukarno was born in Surabaya, Java, on June 6, 1901. One of the first articles he wrote was "Nationalism, Islam, and Marxism," the model for his thoughts and work during his lifetime. During the Japanese occupation in World War II, Sukarno collaborated with the Japanese in return for their support. Immediately upon Japanese surrender in 1945, Sukarno declared Indonesia's independence. Years of chaos followed, until he installed his "Guided Democracy" in 1959 and became a virtual dictator until the coup of 1965. Ousted by Suharto in 1966, Sukarno was isolated under house arrest and died on June 21, 1970.

Sukarno

## Mohammad Hatta (1902–1980)

Born in Bukittinggi, Sumatra, Hatta studied in the Netherlands and graduated with a doctorate in economics in 1932. He then returned to Indonesia and joined Sukarno's nationalist movement. After World War II, Hatta became vice-president under Sukarno, and in 1948, he was made prime minister. He also served as Indonesia's United Nations ambassador. Hatta resigned in 1956 because of disagreements with Sukarno about policies. After Sukarno's fall, Hatta returned to government in various advisory roles.

Mohammad
Hatta

## Megawati Sukarnoputri (1947– )

The leader of the Indonesian Democratic Party (PDI), Sukarnoputri is the daughter of the first Indonesian president, Sukarno. She was raised during the formative years of the new Republic of Indonesia. Sukarnoputri became the first democratically elected chairperson of a rival political party when she became leader of PDI in 1993. In June 1997, she was ousted from this position by military-backed rivals. Since the economic crisis of 1997, she has garnered widespread support, but it remains to be seen if she will lead Indonesia as her father once did.

Megawati
Sukarnoputri

# Government and the Economy

Indonesia is a constitutional republic. In 1945, it proclaimed its independence from the Netherlands, and, in 1949, the Netherlands recognized the sovereign Republic of the United States of Indonesia. Indonesia's federal system was abolished the following year, and the country became a Unitary Republic. Three provisional constitutions define Indonesia's governmental structure. The first one was proclaimed in 1945, the second one was issued in February 1950, and the provisional House of Representatives passed the third in August 1950. In 1959, the constitution of 1945 was reinstated by presidential decree.

## PROVINCES

**Indonesia is divided into twenty-seven provinces, three of which are special autonomous territories: Yogyakarta and Jakarta Raya on the island of Java, and Aceh on the island of Sumatra.**

*Left:* **The former Indonesian president Suharto (*right*) retired in May 1998 in the midst of the Asian economic crisis. He was replaced by former Research and Technology minister, Jusuf Habibie (*left*).**

## Branches of Government

Indonesia has three divisions of government. The executive branch is led by the president, who is elected to a five-year term by the legislative body, called the People's Consultative Assembly. The president does not have a limit on the number of terms he may serve; he appoints and presides over a cabinet of ministers, has wide powers, and can govern by decree in emergencies. The People's Consultative Assembly is made up of 400 directly elected and 100 appointed members, plus an additional 500 legislators. Assembly members represent functional groups, including farmers, business people, intellectuals, women, and regional areas of the country. The assembly meets at least every five years to elect the president and decide major governmental policy. The legislature must approve all statutes and has the right to draft bills for submission to the president.

The judiciary branch hears civil and criminal cases in district courts. Appeals are heard in high courts located in fourteen major cities. The highest court of appeal is the supreme court in Jakarta. One codified criminal law applies to all Indonesia. In civil cases, however, Indonesians are tried under the uncodified customary law (adat law). A governor and local legislative and administrative bodies administer the twenty-seven provinces.

*Left:* Indonesia's armed forces come under the supreme command of the president.

17

## Economy and Industry

The government nationalized industry in the early 1960s. This policy did not work well, however, and the government is now in the process of privatizing industry — that is, selling industrial plants back to independent owners. This policy is intended to attract foreign capital that will increase local employment and revive the national economy.

## Agriculture and Fishing

More than half of the working population in Indonesia is employed in the agricultural sector. Small farms produce rice, cassava, corn, sweet potatoes, coconuts, sugarcane, soybeans, peanuts, tea, tobacco, and coffee. Despite its large agricultural output, Indonesia still imports many basic food products.

An island country with easy access to the sea, Indonesia has long valued seafood and other sea products. Fishing is a part-time employment for much of the rural population. Each year, the sea yields thousands of tons of fish, pearls, and shells. Agar, which is extracted from seaweed, is the most common substance used in laboratories to grow cultures.

*Below:* **Women harvest rice from the fertile paddy fields of Bali. Rice is one of Indonesia's main exports. The archipelago's lowlands are so enriched by volcanic ash that they yield three rice crops a year.**

## Manufacturing

Manufacturing makes up 21 percent of Indonesia's gross domestic product (GDP). Industrial expansion remains a major goal of government development programs. Many existing enterprises are devoted to petroleum refining, textiles, and food processing. Other leading branches of the manufacturing sector include wood products, tobacco, and chemicals. Manufacturing is concentrated in Java.

## Exports and Imports

Most of the produce from plantation estates, such as rubber, tobacco, sugar, palm oil, coffee, tea, and cacao, is exported. Textiles, garments, and footwear are also produced largely for export. Indonesia is also one of the world's largest exporters of plywood. Indonesian imports include consumer goods, raw materials, and fuels. Foreign investments in petrochemical, electronic, light industrial, and consumer products are shaping the economy. Japan is the largest foreign investor in Indonesia.

*Above:* **Kuta beach in Bali is one of the most popular tourist destinations in Indonesia. Tourism is a major industry, employing hundreds of thousands of people in hotels, resorts, and in the transportation and food industries.**

# People and Lifestyle

## Ethnic Groups

Hundreds of years ago, migrations from China, Malaysia, Borneo, Thailand, and other Asian civilizations created a dynamic mixture of more than a hundred linguistic and ethnic groups in Indonesia. Today, more than 300 ethnic groups live in Indonesia, each with its own cultural identity. More than 250 distinct languages are spoken in the archipelago. Dozens of minority groups are scattered throughout the islands. Several million Chinese have migrated to Indonesia over the past few centuries. Other Asian peoples, such as the Vietnamese, escaped their own lands during troubled times and came to the islands. The Dutch, once rulers of the islands, have declined to nominal numbers.

In all their actions, Indonesians respond to an inner need for discipline and self-control. Many art forms are exercises in discipline. The puppets of the *wayang* (wah-yahng) shadow plays present various examples of good and bad behavior. The making of beautiful classic *batik* (BAH-tik) designs involves great patience

### THE CHINESE-INDONESIANS

The Chinese settled in Indonesia well before the arrival of Europeans. Today, the Chinese make up about 5 percent of the total population.

(*A Closer Look, page 46*)

*Below:* **Balinese women dress in traditional finery for a temple festival.**

## TRADITIONAL DRESS

There are over three hundred ethnic groups in Indonesia and just as many forms of traditional dress — ranging from the "almost bare" fashion of the Dani tribesmen to the *batik sarong* (BAH-tik SAH-rong) of the Balinese.
(*A Closer Look*, page 68)

*Left:* A Dani tribesman and his daughter pose inside their home. The people of Irian Jaya have not been influenced by modern civilization, and they still follow age-old traditions in all aspects of their lives, including dress and beliefs.

and concentration. The movements of many traditional Indonesian dances require physical and mental discipline.

# Transmigration

The islands of Java and Madura are amongst the most populous urban areas in the world, with over 200 million inhabitants. In these heavily populated regions, Indonesians endure crowded living conditions, and crime is rampant.

Indonesia has developed a type of voluntary program designed to improve the quality of life for all the people by reducing the strain on severely overcrowded areas of the country. The program permits poor, landless families in overpopulated areas to move to underdeveloped regions and begin a new life with a house, land, and technical assistance. Since the program started in 1950, more than six million Indonesians have relocated with government sponsorship. An additional six million have relocated under the program without government sponsorship.

This effort is essential to a better health standard and the continued prosperity of populous areas, such as Java, an island of more than ninety million people.

## HEALTH STANDARDS

Community health is inadequate throughout Indonesia. Water and air pollution and traffic congestion have rapidly increased with the population explosion. Poor diet, overcrowded housing, lack of sanitation, and contaminated water supplies contribute to the serious health problems facing Indonesians. The government has instituted programs for raising health standards and remedying social problems, such as drug abuse and prostitution.

# Rural Life

In rural societies, families work together in all aspects of life, whether they are harvesting rice or preparing for feasts. The entire village is invited to celebrations. Villagers bring gifts of money to cover costs of preparations. At wedding celebrations, people of the village build a house for the young couple.

In a typical village, the home is an enclosed platform raised ten to twelve feet off the ground. A removable ladder provides the entrance. To keep unwanted visitors out, a family simply draws up the ladder! Outside the house, on a gallery or porch, is a washing area.

## THE TORADJA

The Toradja live in Central Celebes and are rice farmers. They have a fascinating artistic, religious, and social culture.
(*A Closer Look, page 66*)

Ailing or retired grandparents often live with young couples. On farms, women sometimes work in the fields, but most have the job of winnowing grain stalks (separating grain from husks). Rural schools are plentiful, but advanced education in rural communities is still rare.

*Above:* In rural communities, villagers use river water for bathing and household purposes, such as washing clothes.

# Urban Living

The majority of Indonesians do not own automobiles and depend on bicycles and motorcycles for private daily transportation. The neediest live in tin and cardboard shacks on the outskirts of urban areas. Average working families usually live in apartments in the inner city. Like villagers, city dwellers of the same extended family normally choose to live near each other.

Apartments are small and, as a rule, often occupied by two or more generations. In Asian culture, the younger generation takes care of its aging parents. Birth rates are high, with the population doubling in the last generation. Crowding is, therefore, a way of life. Toilet and kitchen facilities are often shared among households in older apartment buildings. Modern appliances, such as televisions, washing machines, and full-size refrigerators, are also shared. Up to the period of upheaval in 1998, however, this situation was improving rapidly.

## WEDDING TRADITIONS

**The legal age of marriage is sixteen for women and eighteen for men, but the government tries to encourage women not to marry before the age of eighteen. In rural villages, however, women still marry very young.**
*(A Closer Look, page 72)*

## Status of Women

Although Islam is the major religion of Indonesia, the country's social customs differ greatly from those found in Islamic states of the Middle East. Most Indonesian Muslim women wear no veils and mix freely with men. In virtually all areas, customary law gives women substantial rights in property settlements, inheritance, and divorces. While technically, as in other Islamic countries, a man may take up to four wives for economic and social reasons, this is virtually never done in Indonesia. The long established custom of arranged marriages has increasingly given way to the Western system of individual choice.

*Above:* The *becak* (BEH-chak) is a three-wheeled bicycle-rickshaw, where the driver cycles in the rear of the carriage. In Yogyakarta, becaks are colorful creations, with tinkling bells and spinning discs.

## Education

The educational system is handicapped by the fact that public education has been available only since 1947. During Dutch colonial rule, the Dutch did very little to encourage higher education. As a result, upon independence in 1945, there were no universities and few primary and secondary schools in Indonesia. Today, although the number of educational institutions has greatly increased, much remains to be done to improve the quality of teaching and the standard of educational facilities.

The country's school system is patterned after that of the Dutch. The secondary school curriculum is divided into three sections: mathematics, languages, and economics. The early 1990s saw the enrollment of almost thirty million Indonesian youngsters into the secondary system, and 1.4 million attended vocational institutes.

## Higher Education

Indonesian universities and colleges now admit about two million students each year. Entrance into secondary schools and universities is highly competitive. Only 10 percent of the

*Above:* **Indonesian children attend six years of primary education, followed by three years of junior and three years of senior secondary education.**

applicants to government universities are accepted. Of the rest, those who can afford it attend private schools. Higher education is available at several institutions, including the University of Indonesia in Jakarta and Gadjah Mada University in Yogyakarta, the oldest university in Indonesia. A growing number of students attend colleges and universities overseas, particularly in the United States, Australia, Germany, and the Netherlands.

## Literacy

In the early days of the republic, about 80 percent of Indonesians aged fifteen and over were illiterate. The new republic's most pressing problem was to contend with growing demands for education and a rapidly increasing population resulting in a large percentage of school-aged children. Today, the law requires all children to attend at least nine years of school. Since independence, Indonesia has successfully met the challenge of providing education to its children, and today, about 90 percent of Indonesian children receive free, compulsory, primary instruction. In the early 1990s, literacy increased to 79 percent.

*Below:* **Muslim schoolgirls head for home after a school day in South Celebes.**

# Religion

Religious beliefs in Indonesia cover a wide range. For almost a thousand years, Indonesia's involvement in maritime trade opened it to cultural and ethnic influences from all over the world. About 87 percent of Indonesians are Muslims, and about 9 percent are Christians. Hindus make up about 2 percent of the population, most of whom live on Bali, which has a very strong Hindu culture today. There are about 1.6 million Buddhists.

In 1945, Sukarno established the Pancasila (pan-cah-SEE-lah), or Five Principles, to guide Indonesians. One of the principles is the belief in one supreme god, whether Muslim, Christian, Hindu, or Buddhist.

# Islam

Islam was introduced to Indonesia by Arab and Malay traders in the ninth century. At the time, Islam appealed to the masses because it taught the equality of humankind, as opposed to the caste system of Hinduism. Today, although the majority of Indonesians are Muslim, Indonesia is not an Islamic state.

To Muslims, Islam is not merely a religion, but a way of life. The five central teachings of Islam include Shahada (shah-HAH-dah), or profession of faith; Salat (SAH-lat), or worship; Zakat (ZAH-kat), or charity; Saum (SAH-oom), or fasting; and Haj (HAJ), or pilgrimage.

*Above:* **Muslim women pray during Ramadan, the Muslim fasting month. These women are wearing special white gowns for prayer.**

# Hinduism

The religious and social system of Hinduism, a development of ancient Brahmanism, is vague, amorphous, and many-sided — all things to all people. Hinduism embraces many beliefs and practices, from the highest to the lowest, often opposed to or contradicting each other. Indonesian Hindus are concentrated on the island of Bali, where many temple festivals are celebrated every year.

## Animists and the Cosmic Order

Animism is the belief in the existence of a soul as distinct from matter. One major belief, especially widespread on Java, is that an all-pervading cosmic order embraces both humans and spirits. It is believed that humans coexist with an unseen world of good and bad spirits. Every aspect of existence must, therefore, be ordered to ensure good and avert evil. Animists consult the *dukun* (DOO-koon), or medicine man, for the auspicious days to engage in all types of business and social activity.

**BOROBUDUR**

**The world's largest Buddhist monument, Borobudur, was built in the eighth century by the Sailendra kings. Today, it still plays an important role during major Buddhist events.**
*(A Closer Look, page 44)*

*Below:* **Three days before the Balinese New Year, Balinese Hindus celebrate Melasti, a ritual purification ceremony.**

# Language and Literature

*Bahasa* (bah-HAH-sah) *Indonesia* is the official language of
Indonesia. It stems from *pasar Malay* (pah-sahr mah-lay), or
market Malay, which contains elements of Chinese, the Indian
languages, Dutch, and English, which was the trading language
of the archipelago during the colonial period. Because Malay was
so widely used at the time, nationalist authorities decided that
Malay would make the best foundation for a national language,
and it was thus designated in the 1945 constitution.

## Dialects

More than three hundred indigenous languages or distinctive
regional dialects are spoken in Indonesia. They all belong to the
Austronesian (Malay-Polynesian) family, except for the Papuan-
based languages of eastern Indonesia. Other major languages
in Indonesia are Javanese, Sundanese, and Madurese. Many
Jakartans converse in *bahasa prokem* (bah-HAH-sah PRO-kem), a
form of slang used among close friends. For the educated elite,
English is the principal Western language, and it is generally
taught in secondary schools and universities.

*Left:* **The ubiquitous
newsstand in
Indonesia sells
all kinds of magazines
about politics, fashion,
and entertainment.
The most popular
newspapers in the
country are** *Kompas,
Suara Pembaruan,
Republika,*
**and** *Merdeka.*

## GREAT WRITERS

One of Indonesia's most outstanding modern poets was Chairil Anwar, who was born in Medan in 1922 and died of typhus at the age of twenty-seven. Early Indonesian writers, such as Sanuse Pane and Idrus, made their mark as early critics of the Sukarno regime. In the early 1960s, Mochtar Lubis, editor of the independent newspaper *Indonesia Raya*, was imprisoned for four years for his attacks on corruption and social decay. The government was particularly outraged by his second novel, *Twilight in Jakarta* (1963), where Lubis portrayed the collapse of revolutionary idealism and morality that took place under Sukarno.

# Literature

Javanese written literature dates from the beginning of the tenth century. It consists of prose and verse renditions of the great Hindu epics. During the Islamic period, historio-mythological compilations were produced in which creatures of Hindu-Javanese legends and Islamic saints were intermingled.

The nationalist movement after World War I encouraged literary activity. The earliest Indonesian novels were published in the 1920s. In 1933, the New Writer literary school was established. It became the major influence for a group of young writers, who created a "superculture" linked with the development of *Bahasa Indonesia* as the national language. Writers of the period reflected the revolutionary attitudes of Indonesians under Japanese occupation. Despite interference and control by the government, Indonesian literature continued to develop.

# Arts

Indonesian art reflects the creativity of a people with a rich cultural heritage and idyllic natural surroundings. Art, like religion, is woven into the patterns of daily life. It is an integral part of celebrations and religious rites, as well as a principal source of recreation and enjoyment. Various Indonesian art forms are based on folklore, but others were developed in the courts of early kingdoms or as part of a religious tradition.

## Foreign Influences

Hinduism and Buddhism have exerted great influence on Indonesian culture. Since the thirteenth century, Arabic countries have also left their mark on Indonesian art through the teachings of Islam. Southeast Asians, Polynesians, the Dutch, and other groups have significantly changed the lifestyle of native Indonesians. Today, Indonesia is a multiracial melting pot.

**RAMAYANA AND MAHABHARATA**

**Two of the most famous Hindu epics are the *Ramayana* and the *Mahabharata*. Many Indonesian dance dramas and wayang performances are based on these epics.**
*(A Closer Look, page 60)*

*Left:* **The *legong* (LAY-gong) is one of the most graceful Balinese dances. Legong performers, usually girls as young as eight years old, dress in elaborate gold brocade wrapped tightly around their bodies and headdresses decorated with frangipani and other flowers. In the legong, two dancers perform in perfect unison with each other, using amazingly controlled and agile movements. One of the most popular legong dances is the *Legong Kraton*, which relates the story of a king who takes a maiden captive and is later visited by a bird of ill omen, which heralds his death.**

*Left:* **The Dayak tribes of Kalimantan are well-known for their singing and dancing.**

## Music and Dance

The famous dance dramas of Java and Bali are based on Hindu mythology. They often feature fragments from the *Ramayana*, *Mahabharata*, and other Hindu epics. Dancers often wear elaborate costumes, and dance actions are controlled and fluid. Some famous dances include the legong, *kecak* (ke-chak), and *barong* (BAH-rong).

To the Indonesian, dancing, which marks almost all special occasions, is more than just recreation. Through dance, people seek the favor of gods and spirits to ward off evil. The dancers seek to lose themselves in music, often wearing elaborate or grotesque masks.

Full *gamelan* (gah-MAY-lahn) orchestras accompany these highly stylized dances. Gamelan orchestras typically feature instruments similar to the xylophone, drums, gongs, and occasionally, stringed instruments and flutes.

### GAMELAN MUSIC

**The sounds of a gamelan orchestra are the most distinctive sounds of Indonesia. Gamelan music originated in Java and Bali and accompanies traditional dance and wayang performances.**

*(A Closer Look, page 54)*

31

# Wayang

The leather shadow puppet show of Bandung is one of the most fascinating forms of Indonesian performing arts. These shadow plays are usually accompanied by a gamelan orchestra. Many forms of wayang exist, including *wayang kulit* (wah-yahng koo-lit), which features flat leather shadow puppets and *wayang golek* (wah-yahng goh-lek), which features wooden hand puppets. Both art forms narrate stories, usually based on one of the Hindu epics. They frequently offer thinly veiled comments on contemporary political figures and events.

# Weaving

Batik is created through a tedious process of waxing and dyeing that originated in Java centuries ago. In the basic batik process, white or light cloth of natural fiber is lightly traced with a design, which is filled in with molten wax and left to harden. The cloth is then steeped in a dye that soaks into all but the waxed areas of the cloth. After the cloth has dried, the wax is scraped away. This process is repeated with different colors and designs.

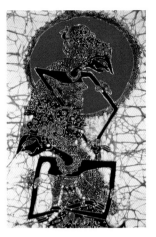

**WAYANG KULIT**

**The batik design above depicts shadow puppets. Wayang kulit, a form of shadow puppetry, is a favorite Indonesian performing art.**
*(A Closer Look, page 70)*

Artists in Java, South Sumatra, and other provinces produce ornate gold embroidery, cloth woven with gold and silver threads, and intricately patterned silks or cottons used for formal dress and artistic performances.

*Ikat* (EE-kaht), which means "tie," refers to the patterned cloth that is chiefly made in the province of Nusa Tenggara. The painstaking process of ikat-making involves tie-dyeing the threads before they are woven. Traditionally, one piece of ikat takes over a year to complete.

## Carving

Balinese artisans fashion elaborate carvings of wood, bone, horn, and stone. Hollowed bones and horns, incised and stained with geometric motifs and stylized figures of animals, hold lime for betel chewing. (In many tropical countries, the center of the seed of the betel palm is chewed together with lime and the leaf of the betel plant.) Wooden stoppers are carved in the form of human heads or birds. Horses of carved bone form the hilts of swords. Tortoiseshell fretwork with bird, reptile, deer, and horse motifs are featured on the tall hair combs worn by the women.

*Above:* **Both traditional and contemporary styles of painting are popular in Indonesia. Bali and Yogyakarta are the art centers of Indonesia, where many masterpieces created by both local and foreign artists are housed.**

*Opposite:* **A woman weaves on a traditional loom beneath a colorful display of completed woven cloth.**

# Leisure and Festivals

Indonesians living in the capital city of Jakarta look forward to the weekends, when they enjoy shopping, watching films, or visiting friends and relatives for a relaxing chat. Watching television is steadily becoming one of the most popular leisure activities in Indonesia. The most popular programs are foreign films from the United States and local soap operas. Many young Indonesians read Japanese comic books and foreign novels translated into Indonesian. Many people also enjoy the game of *congkak* (CHONG-kak), where players take turns placing pebbles in hollows in a wooden board.

Students in many Jakartan schools participate in extra-curricular activities, ranging from sports and religious activities to singing in choirs and playing in marching bands.

Wayang performances are popular social events, where entire villages converge to chat and relax while watching shadow plays of familiar ancient epics.

*Below:* **During public holidays, Indonesians flock to the beach for a fun day with the family.**

## Water Activities

The islands of Indonesia offer unlimited water sports and hundreds of thousands of miles (kilometers) of tropical beaches. Indonesia's underwater coral gardens and fish haunts are world famous. The archipelago attracts millions of tourists each year, and beach resort facilities range from modest open sheds to luxurious beach hotels.

The wide range of outdoor activities includes scuba diving, snorkeling, water skiing, windsurfing, jet skiing, and jet boating in addition to more common activities, such as swimming, sunbathing, picnicking, and fishing. Many marinas provide recreational water vessels of all kinds, from tiny sail craft to sport-fishing motor boats and luxury yachts. School and national holidays are frequent, affording Indonesian families long weekend getaways at nearby beaches.

The legendary waves of the South China Sea and Indian Ocean attract expert surfers to Indonesia. They come from all over the world for the surfing challenge of a lifetime.

*Above:* **Fishing boats, with their characteristic triangle sails, provide an amazing sight in this Bali fishing hamlet.**

# Team and Competitive Sports

The most popular sports in Indonesia are badminton and soccer. Particularly favored by Indonesia's ex-president Suharto, badminton is a favorite sport in Indonesia and throughout Asia. It is a fast-paced, highly athletic game that hinges on deft skills and quick reflexes. Indonesia has dominated this game throughout the 1990s and occupied all the top positions in the 1996 world rankings. Indonesian superstar Joko Suprianto is vaunted as the world's greatest badminton player. His compatriot, Susi Susanti, the defending Olympic champion, is widely regarded as the best female badminton player.

Soccer was first introduced to Indonesia on April 19, 1930, in Yogyakarta. Semiprofessional soccer was introduced in the late 1970s. In 1938, Indonesia became the first Southeast Asian team to take part in the World Cup Soccer Finals. In 1987 and 1991, the Indonesian National Team obtained two gold medals in the Southeast Asian (SEA) Games.

*Above:* **Rudy Hartono is a badminton legend in Indonesia. He has won the All-England Badminton Championship eight times.**

*Left:* **Badminton champion Susi Susanti is one of the most celebrated athletes in Indonesia. She is married to another of Indonesia's badminton legends, Alan Budi Kusama. They won Indonesia's first Olympic gold medals in 1992, the only Olympic golds ever won by Indonesian athletes.**

# Traditional Sports

Indonesians enjoy traditional sports, such as *sepak takraw* (SE-pak TAH-kraw), which resembles volleyball. The object of the game is to keep a rattan or plastic ball in the air with the feet. Two teams of three players compete for the highest score by spiking a ball into the opponent's court using foot play.

The men of Nias Island participate in the dangerous sport of stone-jumping. Dressed in traditional costumes, men exhibit incredible dexterity, daring, and skill as they jump over a stone wall 5 feet (1.5 m) high and 1.5 feet (0.5 m) wide. Stone-jumping was once part of an initiation ceremony for young men.

**COCKFIGHTS AND BULLFIGHTS**

A popular Indonesian pastime is cockfighting, where people root for their favorite roosters. In Sumatra, bullfights are arenas of gambling and sport.

*(A Closer Look, page 48)*

*Left:* On Nias, stone-jumping was once used to train warriors. They wanted to be able to clear enemy walls with a torch in one hand and a weapon in the other.

# Festivals

Many festivals celebrated in Indonesia are based on religious traditions. Other festivals commemorate momentous events in Indonesian history.

On May 25, Indonesian Buddhists celebrate Waisak Day at the site of the Buddhist monument Borobudur and the Mendut temples. This day commemorates Buddha's birth, death, and enlightenment.

Galungan, or the Balinese New Year, consists of ten days of village celebrations that honor departed ancestors. Galungan is celebrated on the first day of the Hindu calendar year, which has 210 days. Evil spirits are driven off by incantations and firecrackers. Cockfighting is a common festivity during Galungan.

In February, Muslims commemorate the birth of Prophet Muhammad, the founder of Islam, with a week-long festival. The largest celebration is held in Yogyakarta. The festival starts with a performance by the sultan's gamelan orchestra. A parade of floats then proceeds from the sultan's palace through the streets, where the sultan distributes rice cakes to the people.

The Ramayana Ballet Festival is celebrated from May through October in the week of the full moon each month.

*Left:* **Schoolchildren are the main participants in the Independence Day parade in Jakarta.**

Performed by a cast of 500 dancers, the festival features a four-episode dance drama version of the classic Hindu epic, *Ramayana*. The performance is staged in the Roro Jonggrang temple near Yogyakarta.

*Above:* **Many Indonesian festivals, such as the Lake Toba Festival in Sumatra, are regional.**

On August 17, Indonesia celebrates its Independence Day with a presidential parade in Jakarta. After the president reviews his troops in Merdeka Square, a parade of floats and a citizens' march entertain crowds of spectators. In the evening, the entire city center comes alive with festive decorations and lights.

The Kesodo Ceremonies in August are celebrated by the Tenggerese at the active crater of Mount Bromo in East Java. Thousands of people climb the walls of the crater and stay overnight to observe the sunrise in the morning.

In mid-October, bull races are held at Pamekasan, Madura. The bulls are adorned with elaborate ornaments, and onlookers are serenaded by the Madurese drum and flute players.

Christmas is celebrated by the few Christians on Batak in North Sumatra and the Minahasa in North Celebes.

# Food

The broad spectrum of cuisine in Indonesia results from centuries of foreign influence. Diverse immigrant populations from China, India, Japan, Thailand, the Netherlands, and Sri Lanka have brought many specialized cooking techniques to Indonesia.

## Favorite Indonesian Dishes

*Satay* (sah-tay) consists of skewered cubes of meat (beef, mutton, and chicken), which are roasted over a tray of burning coal. The meat is dipped in a sauce made from a blend of crushed roasted peanuts, garlic, and chili. Satay is normally served with sliced cucumbers, raw onions, and cubes of rice cake, called *ketupat* (ke-too-paht).

*Soto ayam* (soh-toh EYE-yahm) is a kind of chicken soup popular throughout Southeast Asia. In Indonesia, soto ayam is served with chicken chunks, beansprouts, vermicelli, sliced

*Below:* **Villagers gather for a satay feast.**

*Left:* **This Indonesian woman enjoys a durian snack.**

cabbage, and thinly sliced fried potatoes. *Soto daging* (soh-toh DAH-ging) is beef soup, served with vegetables and noodles.

*Nasi goreng* (nah-see go-reng) is fried rice with chicken or shrimp and chili. It is normally served with a fried egg on top and satay with peanut sauce on the side.

A popular vegetarian dish is *gado gado* (GAH-doh GAH-doh), a vegetable salad with peanut sauce.

## Exotic Fruits

Indonesia has a wide selection of tropical fruits, including starfruit, mango, durian, and jackfruit.

Starfruit, cut into star-shaped slices, is cool and refreshing. Durian has a thorny, green outer skin with creamy white or yellow flesh on the inside. It has a pungent odor. Mangoes are sweet and juicy, with large seeds. Mangosteen is purple on the outside with white, crisp segments inside. The skin of the rambutan is red with spiky hairs. The fruit itself resembles a white grape. *Duku* (DOO-koo) is a small fruit from Sumatra with white, crisp segments inside. Jackfruit is large with a rough skin and fibrous fruit.

# A CLOSER LOOK AT INDONESIA

The word *Indonesia* brings to mind many different images — from the ancient ruins of Borobudur to the modern troubles of East Timor, from peaceful nature reserves to raging forest fires. Indonesian life is as diverse as its thousands of islands, and the country is in a continuous state of metamorphosis.

This section features the unique culture and natural beauty of Indonesia and brings the reader closer to the Indonesian people — their music, art, and way of life. Read about the endangered orangutan in the jungles of Borneo, and learn about Java Man, one of the earliest human remains found in Central Java. Learn about the life of one of the country's greatest leaders, Suharto, as well as the history of the Spice Islands, the products of which enhance the lives of people around the world. This section also features the unique culture of the Toradja and Indonesia's distinctive gamelan music.

*Opposite:* **The Besakih temple complex, which stands in the shadow of Mount Agung in Bali, is considered the foremost Hindu temple on the island. Hindu devotees flock there during religious holidays, such as Galungan.**

*Below:* **The kecak, or monkey dance, is mesmerizing to watch. It is a trance dance, in which a central person is entranced, while surrounding men chant "kecak kecak kecak…"**

# Borobudur

Borobudur is the largest Buddhist monument in the world. It is about 1,200 years old and lies about 42 miles (68 km) northwest of Yogyakarta.

## A Monumental Construction

During the eighth century, King Pancapana of the Buddhist Sailendra dynasty started the construction of Borobudur, which took over one hundred years to complete. During this time, the Sailendra kings were forced out of the Central Java region by kings from Eastern Java, who formed the Mataram dynasty. Although the Mataram kings were predominantly Hindu, the two dynasties cooperated in the completion of Borobudur, bringing skilled artisans from India to help.

Centuries later, Borobudur fell into a state of almost total ruin. It was not until 1907 that restoration began. Today, it is the finest example of Buddhist architecture in Southeast Asia.

*Below:* **Borobudur is situated on the picturesque plains of Central Java.**

## The Structure of Borobudur

Borobudur is built in the form of a stupa, a traditional monument indicating a center of Buddhist influence. The first five terraces of the Borobudur are square and adorned with relief sculpture. At the base of the monument are carvings that show everyday events and punishments in hell. The galleries of the other four square terraces contain carvings that illustrate the life of Buddha and his holy followers. They show stages through which humans must pass before attaining nirvana, or spiritual freedom.

On top of the square terraces stand three circular ones, representing the stages in a person's ascension when he or she is no longer doomed to rebirth. On top of this is the main stupa, with an unfinished statue of Buddha, representing the holiest state a human can attain. On entering the gallery, visitors turn to the left and move in a clockwise direction, keeping the bas-reliefs on their right. This motion is called *pradaksina* (prah-dahk-SEE-nah), or paying tribute to the gods. People who turn right on entering the stupa pay tribute to evil spirits.

*Above:* **On Waisak Day, saffron-clad monks and other Buddhist devotees flock to Borobudur to commemorate the birthday of Buddha.**

# The Chinese-Indonesians

The Chinese in Indonesia have never represented a large immigrant group. They were only one of the many diverse groups joining the largely Malay population. Small Chinese settlements have existed in Indonesia since well before the coming of the Europeans. At first, the Chinese worked in tin mines and on tobacco plantations. Some migrated to West Kalimantan to mine gold or become farmers, but most settled in the trading ports of northern Java.

## Chinese or Indonesian?

For hundreds of years, Chinese people sailed to the shores of Indonesia, fleeing desperate poverty or in search of new markets. The Chinese typically kept to themselves, speaking the dialects of their hometowns and forming their own business associations. The Chinese were entrepreneurial and moved easily into business. Indonesia's rulers were happy that the Chinese

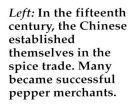

*Left:* **In the fifteenth century, the Chinese established themselves in the spice trade. Many became successful pepper merchants.**

*Above:* **Many modern Chinese-Indonesians are Buddhist devotees.**

distributed goods and loaned money — professions viewed by native Indonesians as undignified. The growth of nationalist ideas among native Indonesians did not readily spread to the more alienated Chinese, few of whom supported the Indonesian struggle for independence. The Chinese were barred from government service and most professions, and Chinese language schools and Chinese characters on signs were outlawed.

The only reliable sign of Chinese identity and of alignment with a Chinese social system is the use of a Chinese surname. Although it was a common practice to adopt an Indonesian surname, identification cards always contained an ethnic label of Muslim, Hindu, Buddhist, Confucian, or Christian, which made assimilation difficult. The words, *pribumi* (pree-BOO-mee), or native, and *keturunan* (ke-too-roo-nan), or nonnative, were common terminology.

Despite the problems of acceptance, however, many Chinese-Indonesians, called *peranakans* (pe-rah-nah-kans), have successfully assimilated into Indonesian society, conversing in Bahasa Indonesia and adopting Indonesian customs.

## THE RIOTS OF MAY 1998

In May 1998, economic problems sparked uprisings against Chinese communities in urban areas, such as Jakarta. The Chinese — seen as rich and well fed — were vilified as usurers and rich landlords. Chinese families fled the country as their properties were ravaged and reports of ethnic Chinese killings increased.

# Cockfights and Bullfights

A chief diversion of Indonesians, especially among men, is so-called "blood sport." During cockfights, hordes of people crowd round the fighting animals, loudly rooting for their favorite rooster. Bullfights are also popular; in North Sumatra, bullfights take place in the afternoon after the workday. Bullfighting is the Sumatran man's favorite pastime.

*Left:* A sharp, metal spur is tied to a rooster's claw before a fight. Cockfights are bloody affairs that generate a lot of excitement in the crowd.

## Cockfights

Cockfights are officially illegal in Indonesia because of the betting involved. Sometimes, the stakes are very high and have led to a person's ruin. Events usually take place in an enclosed building or sheltered area. The fighting roosters are equipped with sharp metal spurs. Selective breeding, training, and the very nature of the birds ensure they will attack in competition. Before a fight, the audience is rowdy, shouting out bets and cheering their champions. When the roosters are let out, the audience quiets down. The combatants spar briefly; feathers fly, claws swipe, and blood drips until one drops to the ground, defeated and dying. When one fight is over, new bets are placed, and the next fight begins.

# Bullfights

High in the mountain jungles of North Sumatra, in the village of Kota Baru, people hold bullfights with a difference. Unlike the bloody bullfights in Mexico or Spain, Indonesian bulls live to fight another day. In fact, they rarely get seriously hurt. In the afternoon, a crowd gathers in a large, flat clearing where four water buffaloes are tethered apart. These black brutes are massive, muscular, and mean. The people, every one an expert, examine each beast critically, placing bets on their favorite bulls.

The show begins when two of the bulls are taken away, and the other two remain to fight each other. There is no barrier between the bulls and the crowd. The bulls lower their great heads, slam their skulls together, and lock horns. The bulls try, snorting and bellowing, to push each other backward. The crowd, only a few feet (meters) away, roars with excitement. Back and forth the bulls go, grinding away at each other. Suddenly, one bull unlocks its horns, turns tail and runs, followed by the victorious bull. Winnings are collected, and more bets are placed hurriedly, as another fight begins.

*Below:* **Two massive bulls prepare to lock horns as the crowd looks on in anticipation.**

# East Timor

The western half of Timor has been a province of Indonesia since the republic achieved independence in 1945. East Timor, however, was colonized by the Portuguese in 1701 and remained a Portuguese colony after World War II. In 1974, a military coup in Portugal led to the establishment of a new government, which sought to rid itself of all colonies of the empire. In August 1975, the Portuguese administration abandoned East Timor, leaving behind chaos and a power vacuum. Various political parties maneuvered to gain jurisdiction. In 1976, Indonesian government troops captured the capital, Dili, and imposed a reign of terror. Australia and the United States urged the United Nations to use diplomatic efforts to end the civil war.

## Indonesia's Twenty-seventh Province

Indonesia's solution to the political unrest was the annexation of East Timor. In this effort, Indonesia relied on the passive support of two countries — the United States and Australia — that were

*Below:* East Timorese, dressed in traditional costumes, dance outside the governor's office during the anniversary of Indonesia's annexation of their country.

interested in oil reserves in the Timor Gap. Indonesia attacked the capital Dili in December 1975. The United Nations and others in the international community promptly condemned the invasion. On July 16, 1976, however, East Timor was officially declared the twenty-seventh province of Indonesia.

A quarter of a century later, the East Timorese are still fighting for their independence. International human rights activists allege that since the invasion, over 200,000 Timorese have been killed by Indonesian troops.

*Above:* **Philippine activists outside the Indonesian embassy in Manila denounce the massacre of the East Timorese.**

## Independence versus Autonomy

In January 1999, in the wake of the economic crisis and unrest of 1997–1998, the Indonesian government announced that it was prepared to grant East Timor either extra autonomy or independence. Since that time, violence escalated and hundreds died, as fighting between pro-independence groups and pro-Indonesian groups increased. In a United Nations-sponsored ballot on August 30, 1999, 78.5 percent of East Timorese voted for independence.

# Ecology and the Burning Forest

Sustainable development of Indonesia's vast natural resources is an important element of the country's economic policy. Indonesia is home to the world's largest tropical forests, which make up 10 percent of Earth's total forestlands. Indonesia's forests form some of the planet's most diverse ecosystems. To preserve this vital resource, Indonesia has placed more than half of these forests — approximately 198 million acres (80 million hectares) — in a permanent trust where little or no commercial development is permitted. Logging and timber operations in Indonesia's tropical forests are run under strict governmental supervision.

*Left:* **In October 1997, Indonesian servicemen tried to put out the forest fires raging across central Sumatra.**

*Left:* **Members of an Indonesian family wear face masks as they ride through the hazy streets of Jambi in Sumatra.**

# Forest Fires

Certain weather conditions, such as El Niño, increase the likelihood of forest fires. In 1997, El Niño, combined with smog created by slash-and-burn methods of clearing farmland, caused severe haze problems in Singapore and Malaysia. At the fourth meeting of the ASEAN Ministers on the Haze, held in Singapore in June 1998, Indonesia proposed an aerial surveillance plan, which would enable firefighters to spot fires early and to take prompt attention to curb their spread. The Indonesian proposal was met with a Malaysian offer of expertise and training and a pledge from Singapore to provide the communications equipment necessary for the immediate transmission of information to agencies on the ground. The United States also did its part by offering $4 million toward the fight for clear skies and clean air and an additional $2 million to assist Indonesia in firefighting operations. The ASEAN countries also resolved to enforce strict laws against open burning and to make legal provisions to discourage landowners from allowing burning on their land.

# Gamelan Music

Gamelan music, an ensemble style of music featuring gongs and xylophones, developed on Java and Bali almost a thousand years ago. It reached its highest development in the court orchestras of Central Java. At that time, the ruling princes of Central Java maintained huge gamelan orchestras, composed of highly trained professionals, to entertain the royal family.

*Above* and *opposite:* **Gamelan music is one of the most distinctive sounds of Indonesia. It accompanies many Indonesian art forms, such as wayang performances and dance dramas, and is a regular feature on special occasions.**

## Gamelan Instruments

Various instruments make up the gamelan ensemble. Bronze bars are complemented by racks of gongs, wooden xylophones, drums, flutes, zithers, and bowed strings. One type of xylophone is the *saron* (SAH-rohn), which consists of bronze bars resting over a trough. It is played with a large mallet. Another type of xylophone, called the *gender* (GEHN-dare), consists of suspended bars over tube resonators.

Large, suspended gongs and drums of several sizes provide the rhythm, or beat, of the music. Horizontal double rows of smaller gongs, or *bonang* (BOH-nahng), played with sticks, elaborate on the main structure of the composition.

A song is performed by male and female vocalists. They are accompanied by a bowed string instrument that originated in the Middle East, called the *rebab* (REH-bahb), and a flute, called the *suling* (soo-ling). Two zithers, the *ziter* (ZEE-tehr) and the much larger *celempung* (che-LEHM-poong), are plucked by the player's thumbnail and dampened with the fingers beneath the strings. A xylophone, called the *gambang* (GAHM-bahng), completes the gamelan orchestra.

## Pak Cokro

One of the most respected musicians in Indonesia is Pak Cokro, whose name is synonymous with Javanese gamelan music. He began as a young court dancer, but his love of music drew him to the orchestra, where he excelled as a talented musician and composer. In the early days of Indonesian independence and through the power struggles of the 1960s, Cokro became popular as a strong nationalist and as director of music for Indonesian National Radio (RRI).

# Java Man

In 1891, the first known fossils of an early type of the species *Homo erectus* were discovered in Java. They belonged to the famous Java Man, the nearest thing to a "missing link" between humans and apes that has been found to date.

## Eugene Dubois

In the late 1800s, Dutch anatomist Eugene Dubois joined the Dutch army as a means of getting to Asia to hunt for the "missing link." Dubois believed that humans had evolved in the Dutch East Indies. With the help of two engineers and fifty laborers, he searched for fossils. In 1891, he found a skull, and a year later, approximately 50 feet (15 m) away from where the skull was found, he discovered a femur. He had discovered Java Man.

*Left:* **Scientists constructed a bust of Java Man based on scant skeletal remains. The extinct Tasmanian Aborigines resembled Java Man, who is characterized by large brow ridges, a robust jaw sculpture, and a small chin. When English settlers invaded Tasmania in the 1800s, the "pure aborigines" of the land were considered less than human and were annihilated. These aborigines (now extinct for over one hundred years), however, were every bit as human as Europeans, Americans, Africans, and Asians.**

Today, Java Man is officially classified as *Homo erectus*, but creationists, or people who believe all things were created by God, claim that the fossils were merely those of giant gibbons. Dubois, however, believes that Java Man was "a gigantic genus allied to the gibbons" — an intermediate between apes and humans.

Since Java Man roamed the Indies about 500,000 years ago, the archipelago received waves of migrants. Some survived to mingle with later arrivals, while others succumbed to annihilation. Many pushed on or were forced out into the Pacific, where they settled on the distant islands of Melanesia, Micronesia, and Polynesia. At about this time, the ancestors of the Papuans of New Guinea and the Aborigines of Australia journeyed on the island highway of Indonesia to reach their final homes.

*Left:* **The Papuans of New Guinea are believed to be descended from Java Man.**

# Orangutans

## People of the Jungle

*Orangutan* literally means "people of the forest." Orangutans live in the wet, hot forests of Sumatra and Kalimantan, the Indonesian region on the island of Borneo. Kalimantan orangutans are reddish brown, while Sumatran orangutans are a pale ginger. The mature male is twice the size of the female and has fleshy cheekpads and a pendulous throat pouch. It can reach a height of up to 4 feet (1.2 m) and weigh up to 243 pounds (110 kilograms). Its voice can be heard up to several miles (km) away.

Orangutans must move through the forest constantly to follow the shifting cycles of flowering and fruiting that determine their diet. Very intelligent animals, wild orangutans know when a particular tree is fruiting, which berries are ripe, and where termites are hatching.

Young orangutans remain with their mothers for about eight years, learning through observation to become expert foragers. Orangutans are not very demonstrative; they generally do not embrace, groom one another, share food, or inspect each other's infants. They appear to communicate through sounds, facial expressions, gestures, postures, and movements.

*Left:* Orangutans swing from tree to tree with long arms that span 8 feet (2.4 m). They are strong but gentle creatures, not prone to aggression. Perhaps orangutans are so beloved by people because of their resemblance to humans.

# Rehabilitating the Orangutan

The orangutan populations in Borneo and Sumatra are in danger of extinction. The rain forests — the orangutan's natural habitat — are quickly vanishing due to logging and forest fires. The black market in young apes has also contributed to their decreasing numbers. Often, poachers kill adult apes to get to their young, which can fetch up to $60,000 each in international black markets. Captive apes are frequently abandoned when they reach adulthood because they are too large and difficult to care for.

Rehabilitation centers, such as Puting Rehabilitation Center in Tanjung Puting National Park (Kalimantan) and Bohorok Rehabilitation Center in Gunung Leuser National Park (Sumatra), rescue captive or orphaned young apes and reintroduce them into the wild. The research station at Tanjung Puting is the site of the world's only long-term orangutan research program. The estimated number of wild orangutans is between 20,000 and 27,000. Hopefully, conservation efforts will protect this gentle animal and revive its numbers.

*Above:* **Nature reservists feed formerly domesticated orangutans that have become malnourished from having been fed on a diet of beer and pizza. The job of rehabilitation centers is to slowly reintroduce these animals into the wild, and, hopefully, teach them to feed themselves from the bounty in the jungle.**

# Ramayana and Mahabharata

The *Mahabharata* and *Ramayana* are the most frequently performed narratives derived from Hindu epics. These epics depict the domination of humans by supernatural forces and symbolic transformations into another realm. They are tales of love and hate, revenge and death, of gods and humans, tradition and change, and of the eternal battle between good and evil. These epics are interpreted on canvas; in traditional dance dramas, such as the barong and the kecak; and in other art forms, such as wayang kulit and wayang golek. In dance dramas and wayang performances, gamelan orchestras prepare special instrumental arrangements, adding the musical accents needed for each performance.

## The *Ramayana*

The *Ramayana* depicts the affairs of the noble Rama and his ancestors. Favorite stories concern Rama's marriage to Sinta, who is later banished to the forest together with Rama's brother. The monster King Rahwana then kidnaps Sinta. She is rescued with the aid of the Monkey King, and, after many battles, returns to the arms of Rama.

## The *Mahabharata*

The *Mahabharata* tells the story of the Bharata dynasty and the kingdom of Hastinapura. It discloses the continuous battle between good and evil, where goodness wins in the end, with the blessing of God and only after many sacrifices. The principal character is Satawati, the charming and beautiful daughter of a poor fisherman. Her father prays that she will marry well and bear a son who will become a wise and great king.

The *Mahabharata* is a highly involved tale with dozens of memorable characters. The plot of the tale consists essentially of a series of complex succession disputes. Most Indonesians know the stories well but still enjoy watching them performed. The *Mahabharata* contains moral and philosophical teachings adopted by many Javanese.

*Above:* **Favored subjects of Indonesian artists are derived from the ancient Hindu epics, the *Ramayana* and the *Mahabharata*.**

*Opposite:* **Each year, the Ramayana Ballet Festival is held on the grounds of the Prambanan temple complex outside Yogyakarta. For four days, large numbers of Sundanese, Javanese, and Balinese dancers perform four episodes of the epic.**

# The Rise and Fall of Suharto

## The Rise of Suharto

Born near Yogyakarta in Java, Suharto was, to the West, the man who saved Indonesia from chaos and anarchy. In the aftermath of the failed communist-led coup of September 1965, Suharto took over the country from anti-Western Sukarno.

Within twenty years, Suharto had restored law and order and achieved a stable, rice-farming economy, leading Indonesians into economic wellbeing. Industrialization followed, providing jobs for the burgeoning population. Redistribution of the people from overcrowded Java relieved areas of Jakarta that were decaying from urban sprawl and poverty.

At the onset of the Suharto administration, Indonesia was one of the poorest nations in the world, with a per capita gross domestic product (GDP) of $70 (U.S. dollars). During Suharto's rule, the population grew from 100 million to 200 million. Before the disastrous collapse of the rupiah in 1998, the per capita GDP had grown to $4,140 (U.S. dollars).

*Left:* **In 1996, Suharto collaborated with the Singaporean government and investors to build Asia's largest tourist resort on the island of Bintan. Pictured are Suharto (*front row, second from right*), with Singapore's prime minister, Goh Chok Tong (*front row, left*).**

# The Fall of Suharto

Despite making great economic progress since the 1960s, Indonesia's political and financial systems were riddled with nepotism, cronyism, and corruption. The devaluation of the rupiah, blamed on the International Monetary Fund (IMF) and Western currency speculators, triggered the collapse of Suharto. In May 1998, total chaos broke out in the capital. Across the country, banks closed, new construction was halted, the rupiah plummeted, and investors and tourists fled the country.

No president, prime minister, or tycoon had ever matched the power of Suharto. His hold on Indonesia was such that talk of his successor was unsettling. Everyone believed he would die in office, having just been elected to a sixth five-year term in 1993. The end of his rule, when it came, was a muted affair, a hastily arranged television broadcast from the presidential palace on May 21, 1998. President Suharto, looking his seventy-six years, apologized for any shortcomings and announced his resignation. His constitutional successor, vice-president Bacharuddin Jusuf Habibie, was sworn in.

*Above:* **On May 21, 1998, after over thirty years in office, Suharto announced his resignation in a television broadcast.**

# The Spice Islands

The Moluccas Islands have some of the few surviving areas of primary tropical rain forest in the world. Land makes up just 10 percent of the area of the Moluccas. The islands are a source of cloves, nutmeg, and pepper — spices that have attracted traders since 300 B.C. Chinese, Indian, and Arab merchants sought the rich lode of spices long before the Europeans did. Archaeological finds have uncovered relics of civilizations dating back 13,000 years.

*Above:* **Nutmeg seeds (*left*) and mace (*right*), the red shell around the nutmeg seed, are major crops of the Spice Islands.**

## Bloody Battles for the Riches

Europeans arrived in the Far East in search of cloves and nutmeg, highly valued as food preservatives and breath fresheners. Spices were also desired for their medicinal qualities — people believed spices could relieve gout, colic, and rheumatism. The great demand made the prices of spices soar. Fleets of adventurers set out from Europe's shores to find the spices and bring them back.

Portuguese spice traders arrived in the Moluccas in the 1500s and brought along military forces to guard their spoils and control the islanders. The Spanish arrived after the Portuguese,

*Below:* **The Banda Islands were at the center of the spice trade during Dutch rule.**

*Above:* **Women dry cloves in the sun. Cloves are often used in Asian and European cooking.**

but none were successful in controlling the spice trade until the arrival of the Dutch, who eventually colonized the entire Indonesian archipelago. The Dutch government barred native ownership and created huge estates to produce a constant and massive spice supply.

By the end of the eighteenth century, however, the spice trade in the Moluccas gradually diminished. The Moluccas Islands were incorporated into the Republic of Indonesia in 1949.

## The Moluccas Today

The Moluccas consist of about 1,000 islands, mostly uninhabited. Just under 2 million people are concentrated on a few of the larger islands. Spices are still the main exports of the Moluccas. Other exports include forest products, fish, and copra (dried coconut meat). Recently, tourists have flocked to the Moluccas, attracted by its incredible sea gardens, idyllic tropical beaches, and wonderful landscapes rich with endemic plant and animal species.

# The Toradja

The Toradja people live in the mountainous areas of Central Celebes. They grow rice on terraced irrigated fields. The Toradja have a distinct architectural style and a unique way of remembering their departed ancestors.

## Toradja Traditional Houses

Constructed entirely of wood and bamboo without a single nail, a Toradja house consists of a rectilinear box of wooden panels set between a frame of sturdy horizontal and vertical beams. This structure is raised on eighteen or thirty-two wooden posts approximately 6 to 18 feet (1.8 to 5.5 m) long. The panels on the outside of some houses are incised with intricate geometric

*Above:* **A carved wooden water buffalo head is a common ornament outside Toradja houses. To the Toradja, water buffalo are symbols of prestige and are the center of ceremonies. The animals are reared for their milk, which is believed to have medicinal properties.**

*Left:* **Toradja houses are characterized by long, swooping roofs.**

designs and symbols of prosperity. A realistically carved wooden buffalo head may be prominently displayed in front, together with rows of buffalo horns from past funeral ceremonies. Perhaps the most striking feature of a Toradja house is its roof, assembled from layers of split bamboo in a great swooping arc, a shape that depicts the curve of a buffalo's horns.

*Above:* **The Toradja bury the deceased in caves and place effigies of the deceased on balconies carved into the cliff walls.**

## Toradja Funeral Ceremonies

The Toradja are famous for the practice of animistic ancient funeral rites. On the death of a noted citizen, a two- to three-week festival period is declared. Guests bring gifts of water buffalo and palm wine to repay favors and other moral debts to the deceased. The festivities include bullfights and dancing. A water buffalo cow is killed, more if the deceased was wealthy. The meat is distributed to the poor of a nearby village. The villagers then form a procession to escort the deceased to nearby cliffs where the family burial crypts are situated in caves. It is common to see a "balcony" on the cave front, with effigies of ancestors dressed in colorful costumes. Succeeding generations of Toradja visit these crypts to pay their respects.

# Traditional Dress

Indonesians dress lightly due to the tropical climate, with temperatures ranging from moderate to very hot. The customary attire for women consists of a cotton blouse and batik sarong; men wear a shirt with a sarong or trousers. Women drape a long strip of cloth over one shoulder. This cloth can be used as a head shawl, or to carry bundles or babies. Men cover their heads with either cloth turbans or fezzes, the latter usually made of velvet. For daily wear, a man may wear a fez of any color except white, which is reserved for hajjis, men who have made the Muslim pilgrimage to Mecca.

## Festive Attire

The daily wardrobe of Indonesians is simple. Festive garments, however, particularly the women's, are elaborate and beautifully made. These garments consist of the finest batik and specially woven cloth intricately brocaded with silk and gold thread.

*Below:* **Minangkabau women wear silk robes with metallic thread woven into the material. They wear characteristic headdresses reminiscent of buffalo horns.**

Indonesian jewelry and accessories consist of necklaces, bracelets, rings, silver hair ornaments, bright plastic beads, gem stones, shells, carved wood, and often fruit pits and nut materials.

## A Dancer's Wardrobe

Dancing costumes are especially stunning. They are made of many layers of elegantly embroidered, rich-colored cloths heavily woven with gold thread. Scarves and long, wraparound strips are accessories used during performances. Colorful umbrellas and woven baskets also accompany the story-based routines. The elaborate costumes extend from head to ankle. Dancers forgo shoes and sandals, performing in their bare feet.

# Wayang Kulit

Wayang, or a performance of actors or puppets, has been a very popular form of entertainment in Bali, Java, and other parts of Indonesia for almost a thousand years. The word *wayang* means "shadow" or "ghost" and describes how the drama is enacted. There are many forms of wayang, including wayang kulit, or shadow puppetry; wayang golek, or wooden puppetry; *wayang orang* (wah-yahng oh-rang), or dramatic dance; and *wayang topeng* (wah-yahng toh-peng), or masked drama.

*Above:* **Wayang kulit performances usually dramatize Hindu epics, such as the** *Ramayana.* **Wayang kulit, however, is often a vehicle for political messages.**

## The Puppet Makers

The puppets are fashioned from fine ivory-colored leather, cut roughly in the shape of the puppet. A stencil is then pinned to the shape, and intricate details are incised on the leather. The figure is then painted white. Stylized features are added in vivid colors, and gold leaf is often used as a decoration. The head is always drawn in a side profile, while the body is turned to the front. The feet face the same direction as the head. The shoulder line projects far out from the sides of the body. A wooden rod or the stem of a split buffalo horn keeps the puppet upright. Its only movable parts are its arms, jointed at the elbow and shoulder. Long, thin rods attached to each hand allow the *dalang*

*Left:* **Puppet makers in West Java are famous for producing exquisite puppets, often valuable works of art for collectors around the world.**

(DAH-lahng), or puppeteer, to control the puppet's hand movements. The size of the puppets depends on whether they represent gods, which are small and slender, or demons, which are usually enormous and grotesque.

## Playing with Shadows

During a wayang kulit performance, the dalang sits behind a white screen. A lantern above his head projects the shadows of his puppet figures onto the screen.

Behind the screen, the dalang lifts the puppets up to take their place in the heavenly world of shadows, moving them according to the characters they represent. Besides manipulating the puppet, the dalang also sings and taps out signals to the gamelan orchestra, which provides the musical accompanying backdrop for every wayang performance. The dalang also improvises the parts for all the characters. One can only marvel at the exceptional skill and resilience of the dalang, especially since every wayang performance lasts several hours, from night until morning.

# Wedding Traditions

## A Suitable Mate

Well-educated women in the late colonial period were expected to contract a suitable marriage that would form a link between two clans. The choice of a partner was a delicate matter. People belonging to the same clan were forbidden to marry. Mediators between the clans would be called upon to decide the merits of the union. Social class was important. Both the bride and groom had to be equal in terms of wealth, intelligence, and physical beauty to ensure the favorable continuation of the clan. In today's society, this ceremonial selection is seldom used among the educated classes. Modern weddings, however, still resemble traditional wedding ceremonies, with all their pomp and ritual.

*Left:* **A Sumatran bride and groom in their elaborate wedding finery.**

# The Complete Ceremony

The complete wedding ceremony has several parts. First, there is the *lamaran* (lah-MAH-rahn), or proposal, then the *peningsetan* (peh-ning-SEH-tan), or engagement. Some time later, a canopy is erected for a special ceremony, called *siraman* (see-RAH-mahn), or bathing. The dukun pours water, strewn with several kinds of flowers, over the bride's head. This is performed at a precise time, because people believe nymphs descend to earth to bathe at that hour; the act is meant to purify the bride. A male counterpart does the same for the groom in a separate room.

*Below:* **A traditional Karo wedding in Berastagi begins with a procession of the married couple and their relatives.**

Two yellow coconuts are tied together, symbolizing the new couple. This ritual expresses the hope that the bride and groom will always stay together. A marriage contract is then signed.

The bridal couple is dressed in elaborate traditional costumes. During the wedding ceremony, the bride and her escort enter from one side of the room, and the groom and his attendant enter from the other. The two processions walk toward each other until almost meeting. The bride and groom throw betel leaves at each other, and the one who gets hit first is deemed to be the dominant partner. Other rituals are also performed: the groom steps on an egg to symbolize fertility, and, in a gesture of mutual love, the couple feed each other, usually from a plate of yellow rice.

# RELATIONS WITH NORTH AMERICA

U.S.-Indonesian relations date back to the earliest days of Indonesia's independence movement in the 1940s, when the United States supported the country's bid to end Dutch colonial rule. Since that time, mutual interests between North America and Indonesia have risen dramatically. Today, as the United States supports the need to stabilize Indonesia's financial and currency markets, the importance of sound policy-making in both Washington, D.C., and Jakarta has never been more important. Before the recession and riots of 1997–1998, Indonesia had provided peace and stability in Southeast Asia, an area that has historically been characterized by war, regional conflict, and instability. Strife in the region cost North America dearly during the first half of the twentieth century, as it lost its soldiers to several wars.

*Opposite:* **The Moluccas were at the center of the spice trade that attracted European interest to the region in the sixteenth century. Christopher Columbus himself was searching for a route to the Indies when he landed on the Caribbean islands in 1492. His arrival marked the beginning of European exploration of the New World.**

*Below:* **Two Indonesian men enjoy a drink of Coca-Cola.**

# World War II

The United States' relations with the Republic of Indonesia began during World War II, when U.S. and Indonesian soldiers fought side by side in the then Dutch East Indies. After the surrender of the Japanese to the Allies, the United States provided diplomatic recognition and assistance to Indonesia.

# Sukarno and the United States

Although he was educated in the West, Sukarno's rule was characterized by antagonism toward the West. In 1959, Sukarno introduced the concept of "Guided Democracy," as opposed to the more liberal Western democracy. During the years of "Guided Democracy," Sukarno's power was dependent on good relations with and balance between the military and the Indonesian Communist Party (PKI), which was gaining strength during that time. Many critics viewed his support of the PKI as a precursor to placing the communists in governmental positions. Others speculated that Sukarno was merely trying to slow the growing power of the communists.

*Below:* **Allied troops prepare to land on the shores of Bali during World War II.**

*Left:* **Sukarno's anti-Western policies incited the antagonism of many Western powers, including the United States.**

## Communism in Indonesia

As early as 1953, the United States adopted a policy that called for "appropriate action, in collaboration with other friendly countries, to prevent permanent communist control of Indonesia." In December 1963, U.S. President Lyndon Johnson decided to withhold economic aid to Indonesia in an attempt to weaken the PKI, which had emerged as the largest mass movement in Indonesia. Sukarno then turned to the Soviet Union for aid. This move angered the United States. The U.S. Congress refused to further assist the Indonesian government, which was nationalizing U.S. business interests in Indonesia. U.S. aid was instead channeled to friendly elements in the Indonesian army — the only powerful non-communist force in the country. With U.S. support, Suharto took over the lead of Indonesia from Sukarno, and the communist threat was averted.

## Defensive Alliances

In 1998, U.S. Defense Secretary William Cohen visited Indonesia and reiterated the important role that Indonesia plays in U.S. military and strategic interests in the Asia-Pacific region. Australia, a strong U.S. ally, supported the United States by signing a major bilateral security treaty with Indonesia. The agreement calls for consultations and consideration of joint responses to military threats to either nation. Although Australia once considered Indonesia its primary security threat, today, the two neighbors regularly cooperate on a variety of political, economic, and defense issues. Today, Australia is the principal external supplier of military training to Indonesia's armed forces.

## Political and Economic Might

As the world's fourth most populous nation, Indonesia is not only a strategic ally of North America in Asia, but also serves as an important stabilizing force in this historically unstable region of the world. Since 1975, Indonesia's economy has grown at an annual rate of 6 percent. The turmoil of 1998 does not diminish the fact that Indonesia is the world's largest exporter of plywood, a major producer of textiles and apparel, and a growing exporter

*Below:* **Indonesian soldiers stand guard outside the U.S. embassy during a rash of riots in the 1960s.**

of footwear, furniture, cement, fertilizer, steel, and glassware. Indonesia is also the world's second largest producer of rubber and the third largest producer of coffee.

## ASEAN and North America

In August 1967, Indonesia joined Malaysia, Singapore, Thailand, and the Philippines to form the Association of Southeast Asian Nations (ASEAN). Because of its size, location, and resources, Indonesia plays a leading role in ASEAN diplomacy, contributing to dramatic increases in trade between North America and Southeast Asia.

Indonesia's rapid economic growth over the past quarter century has given rise to many social and political challenges. Indonesia has to address many domestic issues, such as overcrowding, corruption, and poverty. The United States, itself an economic giant, is uniquely qualified to understand these challenges and lend support. Hundreds of U.S. companies are already helping to bring about change in Indonesian-American business through the sharing of technology, management practices, and knowledge.

*Above:* **World leaders, including President Bill Clinton of the United States (*at podium*) and ex-president Suharto (*on his left*), attend the annual Asia-Pacific Economic Cooperation (APEC) Summit in 1993. One of the most important objectives of APEC is to improve world trade.**

# North America's Business Partner

With a population of over 200 million, Indonesia has become an increasingly attractive business partner for hundreds of U.S. corporations. Since 1967, U.S. companies have invested more than $12 billion in Indonesia's economy. In 1996, U.S. exports to Indonesia amounted to $4 billion, supporting almost 70,000 American jobs. The United States has designated Indonesia as a Big Emerging (BE) Market, making it a priority market for North American firms.

While early investment was predominantly in the energy sector, recent investment has been focused on major manufacturing and service sectors. American products and services are in great demand in Indonesia. Indonesia particularly welcomes U.S. companies that invest in human resources or share

*Left:* **During the economic crisis in January 1998, the value of the Indonesian rupiah against the U.S. dollar began to fall. At that time, many Indonesians purchased U.S. dollar banknotes as an investment because they anticipated the value of the rupiah to fall even further.**

*Left:* **The McDonald's fast-food chain is a favorite among Indonesians. When the company opened its first store in Jakarta, hordes of people crammed inside for their first taste of the famous hamburger.**

technologies. The size and vitality of Indonesia provide a wealth of opportunities for U.S. companies in aerospace, power generation, telecommunications, environmental management, financial services, health care, construction and mining, transportation, and other essential services.

In 1997, U.S. exports to Indonesia totaled an estimated $4.5 billion. The main exports were construction equipment, machinery, aviation parts, chemicals, and agricultural products.

U.S. imports from Indonesia totaled $9 billion and consisted of clothing, machinery and transportation equipment, petroleum, natural rubber, and footwear.

Indonesia's rapid economic growth slowed when the economic crisis hit Asia in 1997. Today, the economy is at a standstill, and factories have closed down. Indonesia faces a crisis that requires determination and confidence by the government of Indonesia to overcome.

## The Economic Crisis and U.S. Aid

During the Asian economic crisis of 1997–1998, the United States pledged to provide humanitarian assistance to Indonesia. The U.S. has significant national security and economic interests in a stable and prosperous Indonesia. It has been actively engaged in international efforts to encourage and support the reforms necessary to restore financial stability to Indonesia. Indonesia's full commitment to these reforms is critical to boost financial confidence.

## IMF Financial Package

Many discussions took place between Indonesian officials and the International Monetary Fund (IMF) on how to strengthen and implement Indonesia's adjustment program. The objective is to restore stability and prevent the financial and foreign exchange crisis from becoming an inflationary crisis.

In November 1997, Indonesian officials reached an agreement with the IMF on an economic adjustment program. Supported by a large, official external financing package, Indonesia is to reform its monetary, banking, and corporate

*Left:* **The Asian economic disaster of 1997 and 1998 resulted in a severe devaluation of the rupiah, which in turn led to unemployment, riots, and the disintegration of the Suharto regime. Many expatriates living in Indonesia fled the country during this period, as violence and unrest escalated.**

sector policies for greater efficiency. The IMF offered $45 million in technical aid to support economic reform and to strengthen Indonesia's social safety net. It offered another $56 million in food and medical supplies to meet immediate humanitarian needs. Aid was also provided to help the approximately 12,500 Indonesian students in the United States complete their studies, so they can return to help rebuild their country.

*Above:* **An East Timorese student demonstrates outside the U.S. embassy for the release of jailed guerrilla leader Xanana Gusmao.**

## Social Unrest

Violence in Indonesia spiraled after the fall of Suharto in May 1998. The fall ended thirty-two years of authoritarian rule and allowed long-simmering but suppressed ethnic and religious tensions to erupt. The government appeared ineffectual in the face of the unrest, as have the armed forces, themselves accused of human rights abuses under the former regime.

The United States has helped many countries in times of crisis and has been asked to quell various conflicts around the globe. Regarding the affairs of East Timor and other troubled parts of Indonesia, however, U.S. policy excludes military assistance.

# Immigration and Emigration

Migration of people between North America and Indonesia is not common. Most North American expatriates (North Americans living in Indonesia) work for schools or diplomatic services. Ethnic problems, such as those that occurred in 1998, have prompted an exodus of expatriates from Indonesia. However, cultural exchange between North American and Indonesian schools continues.

# The Fulbright Program

On July 15, 1992, U.S. ambassador John C. Monjo and Indonesia's foreign minister Ali Alatas signed a bilateral Educational and Cultural Agreement. This marked the culmination of years of intensive effort to establish a fully binational Fulbright Commission to administer the educational exchange program.

*Left:* The Indonesian basketball league is not quite the U.S. National Basketball Association (NBA). However, American Bobby Parks, who lives and plays basketball in Indonesia, has become a celebrity on the Indonesian basketball scene.

The Fulbright Program has been operating in Indonesia since 1952, with encouraging results. The program sends Indonesians to the United States annually for graduate study and research. It has enabled several Asians to teach at U.S. universities as scholars-in-residence. The Fulbright Program also brings to Indonesia American professors, researchers, and graduate student researchers.

## American-Indonesian Influence

The future of foreign relations rests in the schools. Graduate and undergraduate American Studies programs are featured in many Indonesian universities, such as the University of Indonesia in Jakarta and Gadjah Mada University in Yogyakarta, the oldest university in Indonesia.

*Left:* **Increasing numbers of North Americans travel to Indonesia every year.**

The United States Indonesian Society was formed in 1994 to increase awareness of Indonesia among American institutions and individuals. Under an agreement with the Indonesian Ministry of Education and Culture, U.S. students are selected for an intensive eight-week language and general studies program in Indonesia. Eligible applicants are college seniors in all fields of study, including the social sciences.

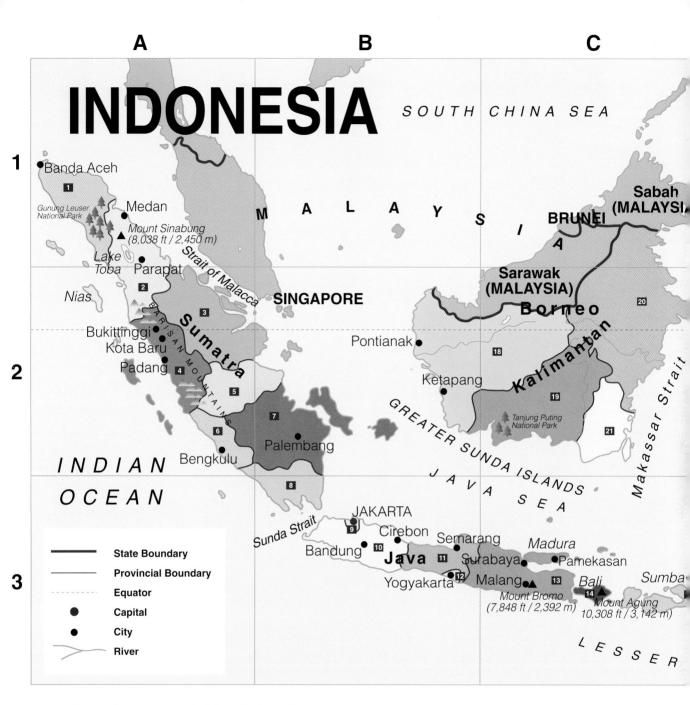

# INDONESIA

SOUTH CHINA SEA

**A** **B** **C**

**1** Banda Aceh

Gunung Leuser
National Park

Medan

▲ Mount Sinabung
(8,038 ft / 2,450 m)

Lake Toba   Parapat

Nias

**MALAYSIA**

Sabah
(MALAYSIA)

BRUNEI

Sarawak
(MALAYSIA)

Borneo

Strait of Malacca

SINGAPORE

**2** Bukittinggi
Kota Baru
Padang

BARISAN MOUNTAINS

Sumatra

Pontianak

Ketapang

Kalimantan

18

19

20

21

Palembang

Bengkulu

7

GREATER SUNDA ISLANDS

Tanjung Puting
National Park

Makassar Strait

INDIAN

OCEAN

8

JAVA SEA

Sunda Strait

JAKARTA

9

Cirebon

Semarang

Madura

Bandung   10   Java   11   Surabaya   Pamekasan

Sumba

**3** Yogyakarta   12   Malang   13   Bali

14

Mount Bromo
(7,848 ft / 2,392 m)

Mount Aagung
10,308 ft / 3,142 m

LESSER

---

— State Boundary

— Provincial Boundary

---- Equator

● Capital

● City

〜 River

---

Agung, Mount C3
Arafura Sea E3–F3
Australia E3–F3

Bali C3
Banda Aceh A1
Banda Islands E2–E3
Banda Sea D3–E3
Bandung B3
Barisan Mountains A2
Bengkulu A2
Borneo C1–C2
Bromo, Mount C3
Brunei C1
Bukittinggi A2

Celebes (Sulawesi) D2
Celebes Sea D2
Cirebon B3

Dili D3

Flores D3

Greater Sunda Islands
 B2–C2
Gunung Leuser National
 Park A1

Indian Ocean A2–A3
Irian Jaya F2

Jakarta B3
Java B3–C3
Java Sea B3–C3
Jayapura F2

Kalimantan B2–C2
Ketapang B2
Komodo Island D3
Kota Baru A2

Lesser Sunda Islands
 C3–D3

Madura C3
Makassar Strait C2

Malang C3
Malaysia A1–C2
Maoke Mountains F2
Medan A1
Moluccas D2–E2

New Guinea E2–F3
Nias A2

Pacific Ocean E1–F2
Padang A2
Palembang B2
Pamekasan C3
Papua New Guinea
 F2–F3

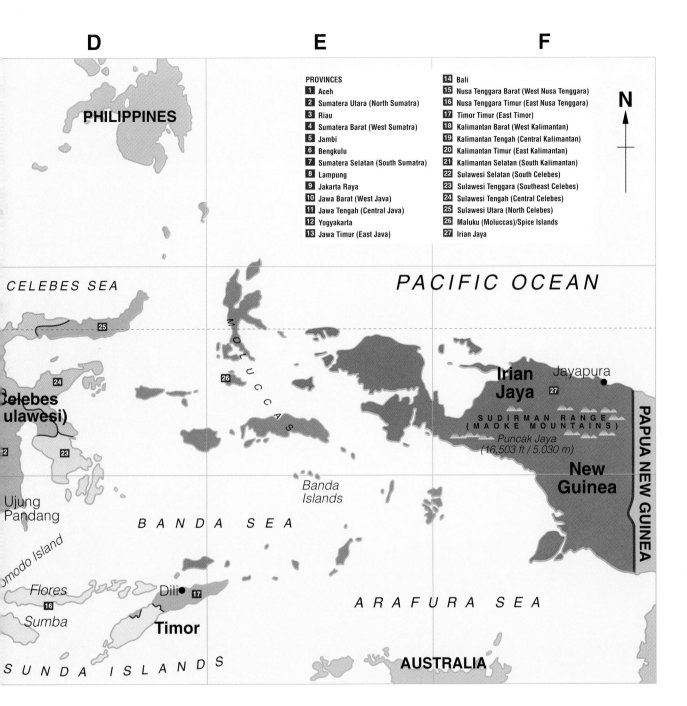

**D**  **E**  **F**

**PHILIPPINES**

PROVINCES

1 Aceh
2 Sumatera Utara (North Sumatra)
3 Riau
4 Sumatera Barat (West Sumatra)
5 Jambi
6 Bengkulu
7 Sumatera Selatan (South Sumatra)
8 Lampung
9 Jakarta Raya
10 Jawa Barat (West Java)
11 Jawa Tengah (Central Java)
12 Yogyakarta
13 Jawa Timur (East Java)
14 Bali
15 Nusa Tenggara Barat (West Nusa Tenggara)
16 Nusa Tenggara Timur (East Nusa Tenggara)
17 Timor Timur (East Timor)
18 Kalimantan Barat (West Kalimantan)
19 Kalimantan Tengah (Central Kalimantan)
20 Kalimantan Timur (East Kalimantan)
21 Kalimantan Selatan (South Kalimantan)
22 Sulawesi Selatan (South Celebes)
23 Sulawesi Tenggara (Southeast Celebes)
24 Sulawesi Tengah (Central Celebes)
25 Sulawesi Utara (North Celebes)
26 Maluku (Moluccas)/Spice Islands
27 Irian Jaya

**N**

*CELEBES SEA*

*PACIFIC OCEAN*

25

**Celebes (Sulawesi)**

MOLUCCAS

26

**Irian Jaya**   Jayapura

27

**SUDIRMAN RANGE (MAOKE MOUNTAINS)**

*Puncak Jaya (16,503 ft / 5,030 m)*

**PAPUA NEW GUINEA**

**New Guinea**

23

Ujung Pandang

*Banda Islands*

*B A N D A   S E A*

Komodo Island

*Flores*

16

*Sumba*

Dili 17

**Timor**

*A R A F U R A   S E A*

*S U N D A   I S L A N D S*

**AUSTRALIA**

Parapat A1
Philippines D1
Pontianak B2
Puncak Jaya F2

Sabah (Malaysia) C1
Sarawak (Malaysia)
   C1–C2
Semarang B3
Sinabung, Mount A1
Singapore B2
South China Sea B1–C1
Strait of Malacca A2
Sudirman Range F2
Sulawesi D2

Sumatra A1–B2
Sumba D3
Sumbawa C3
Sunda Strait B3
Surabaya C3

Tanjung Puting National
   Park C2
Timor D3
Toba, Lake A1

Ujung Pandang D3

Yogyakarta B3

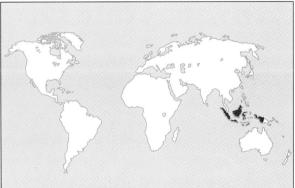

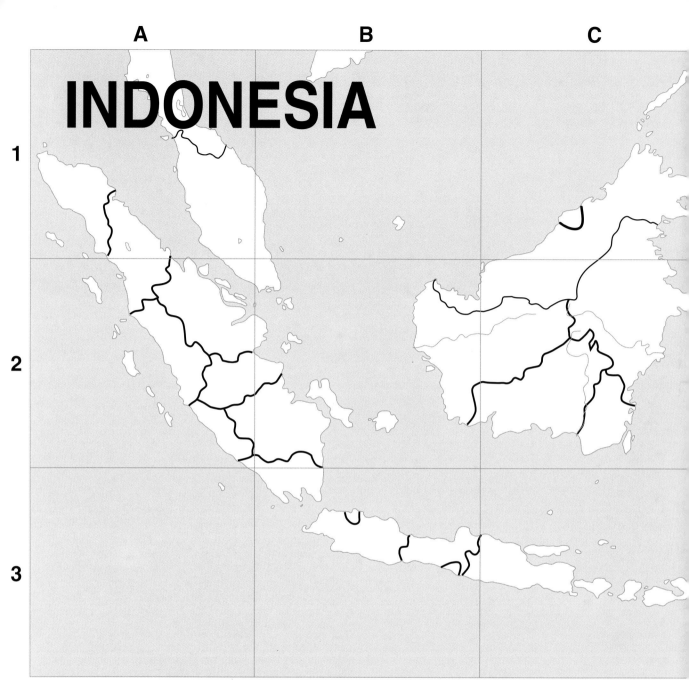

# How Is Your Geography?

Learning to identify the main geographical areas and points of a country can be challenging. Although it may seem difficult at first to memorize the locations and spellings of major cities or the names of mountain ranges, rivers, deserts, lakes, and other prominent physical features, the end result of this effort can be very rewarding. Places you previously did not know existed will suddenly come to life when referred to in world news, whether in newspapers, television reports, or other books and reference sources. This knowledge will make you feel a bit closer to the rest of the world, with its fascinating variety of cultures and physical geography.

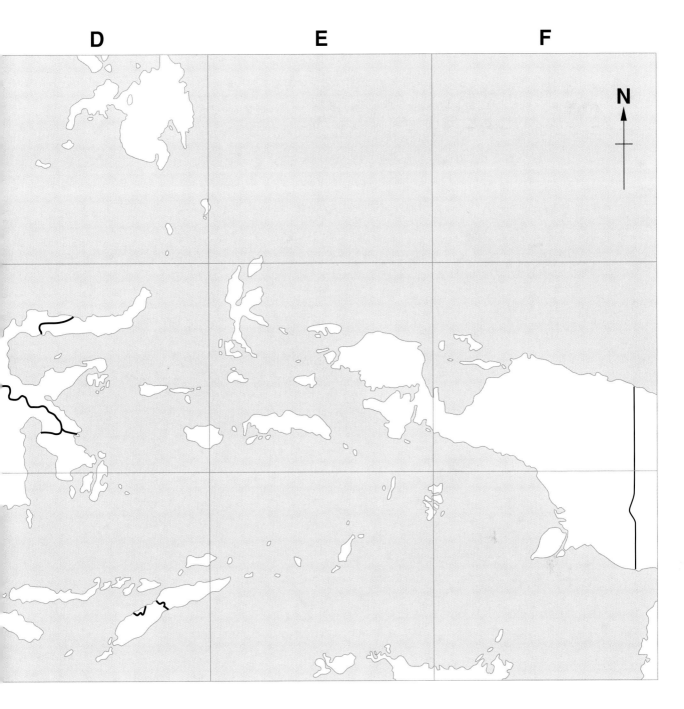

Used in a classroom setting, the instructor can make duplicates of this map using a copy machine. (PLEASE DO NOT WRITE IN THIS BOOK!) Students can then fill in any requested information on their individual map copies. Used one-on-one, the student can also make copies of the map on a copy machine and use them as a study tool. The student can practice identifying place names and geographical features on his or her own.

# Indonesia at a Glance

**Official Name**          Republic of Indonesia

**Capital**                Jakarta

**Official Language**      Bahasa Indonesia

**Population**             216 million (1999 estimate)

**Land Area**              741,052 square miles (1,919,824 square km)

**Major Islands**          Irian Jaya, Java, Kalimantan, Sulawesi, Sumatra,

**Highest Point**          Puncak Jaya 16,503 feet (5,030 m)

**Largest Lake**           Toba 442 square miles (1,145 square km)

**Provinces**              Aceh, Bali, Bengkulu, Irian Jaya, Jakarta Raya, Jambi, Jawa Barat, Jawa Tengah, Jawa Timur, Kalimantan Barat, Kalimantan Selatan, Kalimantan Tengah, Kalimantan Timur, Lampung, Maluku, Nusa Tenggara Barat, Nusa Tenggara Timur, Riau, Sulawesi Selatan, Sulawesi Tengah, Sulawesi Tenggara, Sulawesi Utara, Sumatera Barat, Sumatera Selatan, Sumatera Utara, Timor Timur, Yogyakarta

**Major Cities**           Bandung, Jakarta, Malang, Medan, Padang, Palembang, Semarang, Surabaya, Ujung Pandang

**Principal Ethnic Groups**  Acehnese, Balinese, Batak, Dani, Javanese, Minangkabau, Sasak, Sundanese

**Famous Leaders**         Sukarno (1901–1970)

                           Mohammad Hatta (1902–1980)

                           Suharto (1921– )

**Important Anniversary**  National Independence Day (August 17)

**Major Religions**        Buddhism, Christianity, Hinduism, Islam

**Currency**               Rupiah (8,750 rupiah = U.S. $1 as of 1999)

*Opposite:* Jakarta is the economic and political center of Indonesia. It is also one of the most populous cities in the world, with about nine million people.

# Glossary

## Indonesian Vocabulary

*Bahasa* (bah-HAH-sah) *Indonesia*: the official language of Indonesia.

*bahasa prokem* (bah-HAH-sah PRO-kem): a form of slang used in Jakarta.

*bajaj* (BAH-jaj): a three-wheeled vehicle used as public transportation.

*barong* (BAH-rong): a Balinese dance

*batik* (BAH-tik): a patterned cloth made using a wax and dye method.

*batik sarong* (BAH-tik SAH-rong): a patterned cloth worn at the waist.

*becak* (BEH-chak): a three-wheeled bicycle-rickshaw.

*bonang* (BOH-nahng): a small gong.

*celempung* (che-LEHM-poong): a zither.

*congkak* (CHONG-kak): a game where players take turns placing pebbles in hollows on a wooden board.

*dalang* (DAH-lahng): a puppeteer.

*duku* (DOO-koo): a small, white fruit.

*dukun* (DOO-koon): a medicine man.

*gado gado* (GAH-doh GAH-doh): an Indonesian vegetable salad.

*gambang* (GAHM-bahng): a type of xylophone in a gamelan orchestra.

*gamelan* (gah-MAY-lahn): a form of music developed in Java and Bali.

*gender* (GEHN-dare): a xylophone comprising suspended bars.

*ikat* (EE-kaht): a patterned cloth, where threads are tie-dyed before weaving.

*kecak* (ke-chak): a Balinese trance dance.

*ketupat* (ke-too-paht): a rice cake.

*keturunan* (ke-too-roo-nan): non-native.

*lamaran* (lah-MAH-rahn): proposal.

*legong* (LAY-gong): A Balinese dance performed by young girls.

*nasi goreng* (nah-see go-reng): fried rice.

*pasar Malay* (pah-sahr mah-lay): market, or colloquial, Malay.

*peningsetan* (peh-ning-SEH-tan): an engagement ceremony.

*peranakans* (pe-rah-nah-kans): Chinese people who have adopted Malay language and customs.

*pradaksina* (prah-dahk-SEE-nah): paying tribute to the gods.

*pribumi* (pree-BOO-mee): native.

*rebab* (REH-bahb): a stringed instrument.

*saron* (SAH-rohn): a type of xylophone.

*satay* (sah-tay): skewered meat grilled over charcoal.

*sepak takraw* (SE-pak TAH-kraw): a rattan ball game.

*siraman* (see-RAH-mahn): a bathing ceremony in Indonesian weddings.

*soto ayam* (soh-toh EYE-yahm): chicken soup.

*soto daging* (soh-toh DAH-ging): beef soup.

*suling* (soo-ling): a flute

*wayang* (wah-yahng): drama.

*wayang golek* (wah-yahng goh-lek): wooden puppetry.

*wayang kulit* (wah-yahng koo-lit): shadow puppetry.

*wayang orang* (wah-yahng oh-rang): dramatic dance.

*wayang topeng* (wah-yahng toh-peng): masked drama.

*ziter* (ZEE-tehr): a type of zither.

# English Vocabulary

**amorphous:** without a definite form.

**annexation:** the incorporation of a territory into another territory.

**archipelago:** a chain of islands.

**assimilation:** the process whereby a minority group is culturally absorbed into the larger, main ethnic group.

**auspicious:** favorable; promising success.

**autonomous:** having self-government; not being controlled by others.

**charismatic:** charming; able to inspire and influence others.

**creationists:** people who believe the creation of the universe happened according to the Bible.

**durian:** a pungent fruit with a green, thorny outer skin.

**El Niño:** an abnormal weather condition that affects many parts of the world every few years. It is caused by the raising of temperatures of the oceans along the west coast of South America.

**endemic:** plants or animals that are native to a particular region.

**entrepreneurial:** business-minded and not afraid to take risks.

**esoteric:** understood or practiced by a small group of people.

**expounding:** explaining or proclaiming.

**genus:** a category, class, type, or kind.

*Homo erectus*: upright, apelike creatures that lived on Earth half a million years ago.

**idealism:** a belief derived from a conception of things as they should be.

**idyllic:** picturesque; romantic.

**incised:** cut into or engraved.

**ingenious:** innovative, clever, resourceful.

**integral:** essential.

**inundated:** overwhelmed or engulfed by a great quantity of something, such as water.

**metamorphosis:** transformation; a change in structure, form, substance, etc.

**nirvana:** the Buddhist concept of complete spiritual freedom.

**nominal:** a very small number.

**nymphs:** mythical nature maidens believed to reside in mountains, trees, and rivers.

**orangutan:** a large, tree-dwelling ape native to Borneo and Sarawak.

**pendulous:** hanging loosely.

**pluralistic:** having many groups — with different religious beliefs, ethnicities, and languages, existing together in one place.

**pungent:** sharp and strong, usually referring to a smell.

**rambutan:** a small fruit that resembles a white grape with a red, hairy outer skin.

**rampant:** spreading uncontrollably.

**relinquished:** gave something up that was desirable.

**rudimentary:** basic, elementary, underdeveloped.

**sovereignty:** rule or political authority.

**spectrum:** a wide range.

**stance:** an attitude, thinking, or position with regard to a particular situation.

**succumbed:** surrendered.

**synonymous:** having the nature of or being equivalent to.

**ubiquitous:** present everywhere.

**usurers:** people who lend money at a high interest.

**vilified:** defamed; used slanderous language to refer to someone.

# More Books to Read

*East Timor: Island in Turmoil. World in Conflict* series.  Taro McGuinn (Lerner)

*The Exotic Kitchens of Indonesia: Recipes from the Outer Islands.*  Copeland Marks (M. Evans & Co.)

*Indonesia. Cultures of the World* series.  Gouri Mirpuri (Marshall Cavendish)

*Indonesia. Enchantment of the World* series.  Sylvia McNair (Children's Press)

*Indonesia. Festivals of the World* series.  Elizabeth Berg (Gareth Stevens)

*Indonesia. Major World Nations* series.  Garry Lyle (Chelsea House)

*Indonesia Handbook (2nd Edition).*  Joshua Eliot, Jane Bickersteth, Liz Capaldi, and John Aglionby (NTC Publishing Group)

*Indonesia, Thailand, and Cambodia. Ancient and Living Cultures* series.  Mira Bartok and Christine Ronan (HarperCollins)

*Pak in Indonesia. My Future* series.  Alain Cheneviere (Lerner)

*Volcanoes, Betjaks, and 'Dragons': Let's Travel to Indonesia Together. Windows on the World* series.  Jeannette P. Windham (Global Age Publishing)

# Videos

*Fighting Arts of Indonesia: Combat Sec.* (Paladin Press)

*Indonesia.* (Lonely Planet)

*Indonesia: Jeweled Archipelago.* (Ivn Entertainment)

# Web Sites

www.buddhanet.net/boro.htm

www.pacificnet.net/gamelan/wayangbali.html

www.indonesia.net/Facts.htm

www.indonesia.net/History.htm

Due to the dynamic nature of the Internet, some web sites stay current longer than others. To find additional web sites, use a reliable search engine with one or more of the following keywords to help you locate information about Indonesia. Keywords: *Bali, Borobudur, Jakarta, komodo, orangutan, satay, Suharto, Sukarno, wayang.*

# Index

Aceh 16, 29
Africans 56
agriculture 7, 11, 18, 62
  rice 7, 18, 62, 66
Allied forces 12, 76
animals 9, 65
  komodo dragon 9
apartments 23
Arabs 26, 64
archipelago 5, 6, 7, 10, 11, 20,
  21, 28, 34
architecture 44, 66
armed forces 83
arts 30
  carving 33
Asia 7, 14, 56, 62, 78, 81
Asia-Pacific Economic
  Cooperation (APEC) 79
Association of Southeast
  Asian Nations (ASEAN)
  13, 53, 79
Australia 6, 25, 50, 57, 78

Bali 5, 7, 18, 19, 20, 21, 27, 30,
  31, 33, 35, 38, 43, 54, 70, 76
Banda Islands 64
batik 21, 32, 68
beach 7, 11, 19, 34, 35, 65
Bengkulu 12
betting 48
Borneo 6, 7, 8, 9, 20, 43, 59
Borobudur 27, 38, 43, 44, 45
Brunei 6, 13
bullfighting 37, 48, 49, 67

Celebes 6, 9
  Central Celebes 66
  North Celebes 39
  South Celebes 25
China 6, 10, 11, 20, 40, 83
Chinese-Indonesians 20,
  46, 47

class 72
climate 8
  El Niño 8, 53
Clinton, Bill 79
cockfighting 37, 38, 48
Coen, Jan Pieterszoon 11
communism 62, 76, 77
corruption 14, 63
culture 7, 11, 18, 22, 27, 29,
  30, 43
currency 63
  rupiah 14, 62, 63, 82

dalang 70, 71
dance 5, 21, 23, 30, 31, 38, 39,
  43, 50, 54, 60, 69, 70
  barong 31, 60
  kecak 31, 43, 60
  legong 30
Dili 50, 51
dukun 27, 73
durian 41
Dutch 7, 10, 12, 13, 15, 16,
  24, 25, 30, 40, 56, 64,
  65, 75
Dutch East India
  Company 11

East Timor 14, 43, 50, 51, 83
economic crisis 13, 14, 15, 16,
  51, 81, 82
economy 14, 16, 18, 78, 80, 81
education 11, 22, 24
  universities 24, 25, 85
employment 18
entertainment 70
Europe 11, 64
exports 19, 79

farmers 8, 46
festivals 20, 27, 34, 38, 39, 67
fishing 18

flag 5
Flores 7
food 40
forest fires 8, 43, 52, 53
funerals 67

gamelan 31, 38, 43, 54, 60, 71
geography 6
Germany 25
government 16, 83
  constitution 16
  House of
    Representatives 16
  Indonesian army 14, 77
  military 13, 15, 17, 76, 78
  Pancasila
    (Five Principles) 26
  parliament 13
  People's Consultative
    Assembly 16

Habibie, Bacharuddin Jusuf
  14, 16, 63
Hatta, Mohammad 12, 15
health 11, 21
history
  Dutch rule (see Dutch)
  Ethical Policy 11
  Guided Democracy 13,
    15, 76
  independence 5, 11, 12, 15,
    16, 24, 29, 38, 39, 47, 50,
    51, 54, 75
  Majapahit kingdom 10
  Mataram dynasty 10, 44
  Portuguese 10, 14, 50, 64
  Republic of Indonesia 5, 12,
    15, 16, 65, 76
  Sailendra dynasty 27, 44

ikat 33
immigration 84

imports 19
India 6, 7, 10, 11, 40, 44
Indian Ocean 5, 35
industry 5, 18
International Monetary Fund (IMF) 14, 63, 75, 82
Irian Jaya 6, 7, 13, 21
  Dani 21

Jakarta 5, 6, 11, 14, 17, 25, 28, 29, 34, 38, 39, 47, 62, 75, 81, 85, 90
Jakarta Raya 16
Japan 19, 40
  Japanese occupation 15, 29
Java 6, 7, 8, 15, 16, 19, 21, 27, 31, 33, 46, 54, 56, 62, 70
  Central Java 10, 43, 44, 54
  East Java 39
  West Java 70
Java Man 10, 43, 56, 57

Kalimantan 6, 31, 58, 59
  Dayak 31
  West Kalimantan 46
Kuta beach 19

Lake Toba 39
language 20
  Bahasa Indonesia 28, 29, 47
  bahasa prokem 28
leisure 34
literature 29

Madura 39
Mahabharata 30, 60
Malaysia 6, 8, 10, 13, 14, 20, 53, 79
manufacturing 19, 80
Medan 14
Middle East 10, 11, 54
Moluccas 6, 11, 64, 65, 75
Mount Agung 43
Mount Bromo 39
Mount Sinabung 6
music 31, 38, 43, 54

natural resources 52
New Guinea 6, 21, 57
Nias 37

orangutan 9, 43, 58, 59

Pacific Ocean 5
Papua New Guinea 6
peranakans 47
Philippines 6, 13, 79
plants 9, 65
political parties
  Indonesian Communist Party (PKI) 76, 77
  Indonesian Democratic Party (PDI) 15, 17
  Indonesian Nationalist Party (PNI) 12
  Sekber GOLKAR 17
  United Development Party 17
pollution 21
population 21
poverty 14, 46, 62

rain forest 5, 8, 11, 64
Ramayana 30, 31, 38, 60, 70
religion 23, 26, 30
  animism 27, 67
  Buddhism 10, 26, 27, 30, 38, 44, 45, 47
  Christianity 17, 26, 39, 47
  Hinduism 27
  Islam 10, 15, 23, 26, 29, 30
riots 13, 14, 36, 47, 78, 82

Singapore 6, 8, 13, 53, 62, 79, 82
social problems 21
South China Sea 5, 35
Southeast Asia 5, 13, 30, 36, 40, 44, 75, 79
Spice Islands 11, 43, 64, 75
spice trade 10, 46, 64, 65, 75
spices 11, 64, 65
  cloves 11, 64, 65

mace 64
nutmeg 11, 64
sports 36
  badminton 36
  sepak takraw 37
  soccer 36
  stone-jumping 37
Sri Lanka 40
Suharto 13, 14, 15, 16, 36, 43, 62, 63, 77, 79, 82, 83
Sukarno 12, 13, 15, 26, 29, 62, 76
Sukarnoputri, Megawati 15
Sumatra 6, 7, 8, 9, 12, 15, 16, 23, 29, 37, 39, 41, 43, 52, 53, 58, 59, 72
  North Sumatra 39, 48
  South Sumatra 33
Sunda Islands 9
Surabaya 15
Susanti, Susi 36

technology 79
Thailand 13, 14, 20, 40, 79
Toradja 43, 66, 67, 69
tourism 5, 7, 11, 19, 35, 65
trade 10, 11, 13, 26, 46, 64, 65, 75, 79
transportation 5, 19

unemployment 14, 82
United Nations 13, 14, 15, 50, 51
United States 13, 25, 34, 50, 53, 75, 76, 77, 78, 79, 80, 81, 82, 83, 85

wayang 21, 30, 31, 32, 54, 60, 70
wayang kulit 32, 60, 70, 71
weddings 22, 23, 72, 73
women 23, 68, 69, 72
World War II 5, 12, 15, 76

Yogyakarta 13, 16, 23, 25, 33, 36, 38, 39, 44, 60, 62, 85